D0920439

The Spy Who Tried to Stop a War

The Spy Who Tried to Stop a War

Katharine Gun and the Secret Plot to Sanction the Iraq Invasion

Marcia and Thomas Mitchell

WILLIAM
COLLINS

William Collins
An imprint of HarperCollins*Publishers*
1 London Bridge Street
London SE1 9GF

WilliamCollinsBooks.com

First published in Great Britain in 2019 by William Collins

Previously published as *The Spy Who Tried to Stop a War: Katharine Gun and the Secret Plot to Sanction the Iraq Invasion* in the United States by Polipoint Press in 2008

1

Copyright © Marcia and Thomas Mitchell 2008; additional materials 2019

Marcia and Thomas Mitchell assert the moral right to be identified as the authors of this work in accordance with the Copyright, Designs and Patents Act 1988

A catalogue record for this book is available from the British Library

ISBN 978-0-00-834856-4

All rights reserved. No part of this publication may be reproduced, stored in a retrieval system, or transmitted, in any form or by any means, electronic, mechanical, photocopying, recording or otherwise, without the prior permission of the publishers.

This book is sold subject to the condition that it shall not, by way of trade or otherwise, be lent, re-sold, hired out or otherwise circulated without the publisher's prior consent in any form of binding or cover other than that in which it is published and without a similar condition including this condition being imposed on the subsequent purchaser.

Typeset in Bembo by Palimpsest Book Production Ltd, Falkirk, Stirlingshire

Printed and bound in Great Britain by CPI Group (UK) Ltd, Croydon CR0 4YY

MIX
Paper from
responsible sources

FSC
www.fsc.org **FSC™ C007454**

This book is produced from independently certified FSC™ paper
to ensure responsible forest management.

For more information visit: www.harpercollins.co.uk/green

For daughter Kristin and sons Alan and Jay, and for their
loved ones – which makes them ours as well

And for Paul and Jan Harwood,
Katharine's remarkable parents

It was a decision of conscience in a world where nobody celebrates that. She will go down in history as a hero of the human spirit.

– SEAN PENN

We are going to be in a very dangerous situation as a country if people feel they can simply spill out secrets or details of security operations, whether false or true actually, and get away with it.

– TONY BLAIR

CONTENTS

FOREWORD TO THIS EDITION

The consequences of the invasion and of the conflict within Iraq which followed are still being felt in Iraq and the wider Middle East, as well as in the UK. It left families bereaved and many individuals wounded, mentally as well as physically.
> – 'The Chilcot report' Executive Summary, 2016

Chilcot has shone a light on what happened, but it is clear there are still bits of the puzzle that are missing. Now that we know better, will we do better?
> – Katharine Gun, *Guardian*, 8 July 2016

Gun will not go quietly. Her trial . . . will rehash the war's legality.
> – *Time* Magazine Europe, 2 February 2004

O**N 6 JULY** 2016 – thirteen years after Katharine Gun was arrested for violating the Official Secrets Act, eight years after this book was first published, and seven years after the official UK Iraq Inquiry was launched – a comprehensive government report made worldwide headlines. In twelve volumes totalling 2.6 million words, the inquiry report concluded that the Iraq War was unnecessary, was based on questionable intelligence, and resulted in a chaotic, painful aftermath – all of which were avoidable.

Relevant to this story, Sir John Chilcot's investigating committee concluded that the legality of military action taken by then-US President George Bush and then-UK Prime Minister Tony Blair was questionable and never satisfactorily determined. From January to March 2003, a series of conflicting advisories and decisions revealed shady machinations fuelling Bush's passionate pursuit of the grand prize: a sanctioned war and the removal of Saddam Hussein.

While two heads of state, two of the most powerful men on the planet, secretly plotted the invasion of Iraq to topple Saddam, a young British woman was among those who suspected that the two were set on war – an unnecessary, possibly illegal, war – despite repeated claims to the contrary. Katharine Gun enthusiastically marched against the invasion, along with thousands of others. But for her, marching was not enough.

It's been said that Katharine Gun remains a moral compass for the United Kingdom – someone who was willing to put her own interests behind those of her country and of the world. Fearful that the United Kingdom would launch an illegal war, the British secret service officer risked her freedom and her future in an effort to derail that war and to save lives certain to be lost. She did so by blowing the whistle on a United States spy operation against the UN Security Council (UNSC), an operation designed to ensure that it voted for war. Some called the operation blackmail; others, US 'dirty tricks'. By whatever name, it was unlawful.

At the time, the UNSC was considering a highly controversial resolution to legitimize war against Iraq. Truth, made public by Katharine's whistle, ended the US National Security Agency spy operation and hopes for legalizing the war.

Where the Crown Prosecution Service's most distinguished practitioners wanted to make the criminal case against Katharine about sharing secrets, Katharine wanted it to be about the secrets themselves. She wanted the public to understand what our governments were doing, and who would suffer as a result. She was deeply concerned about the multitude of deaths that would result from an unnecessary war. Her defence, that she believed the Iraq War was illegal, would – years later – be supported by excerpts from the Chilcot report.[1]

But five years would pass before the inquiry would be initiated.

When it was complete, the historic, voluminous document substantiated what Katharine and many others had believed all along – that after the 9/11 World Trade Center tragedy, George Bush determined to get rid of Saddam Hussein and then dragged a reluctant Blair along with him. Of special interest was the release of declassified correspondence between Downing Street and the White House. The cosy exchange of thirty-one letters concerning a proposed invasion of Iraq revealed the truth of the matter. Writing in July of 2002, eight months prior to the invasion – Blair told Bush that, 'I will be with you, whatever.' A mountain of criticism has been heaped upon the former prime minister for fulfilling his risky promise. He is still widely accused of having followed the wrong man into a wrong war.

In fairness, Blair had earlier supported containment as the way to handle threats from Iraq, and he was concerned about what would happen if military action were precipitously undertaken. The report concluded that he was innocent of inventing or distorting evidence to support the war – but that he had indeed weakened and acquiesced to Bush, and that he was responsible for ill-fated decision-making and its ultimate result. In a heated and nearly tearful response, Blair defended his honour, insisting that he had not been a US pawn, that he 'did not mislead [his] country.'

Regardless, it is impossible for this author to reconcile the report's findings with Blair's overarching denial: 'What I cannot do and will not do is say we took the wrong decision.' The world believes otherwise.

Strangely silent in the debate – both during Katharine's case and after the monumental report was released – was the United States. In July of 2016, that country was distracted by the nastiest, most vicious election campaign in its history. The annoying 'Iraq issue' neatly folded into the campaign only as a political weapon: Which candidate had supported the 2003 invasion, and which had not? Still, many American lawmakers regret having supported the invasion.

In *The Restless Wave*, published shortly before his 2018 death, US Senator John McCain wrote that the Iraq War 'can't be judged as anything other than a mistake'. One of the most hawkish Senate Republicans, he had been firmly in favour of the invasion. Later, he took full responsibility for 'my share of the blame for it'. Hillary Clinton, a Democratic senator from 2001–2009, apologized during the 2016 presidential campaign for her previous aye vote in Congress, for having been deceived by the surround-sound of political rhetoric deafening Capitol Hill.

What is easy to miss in the continuing flurry of political hindsight is what Katharine Gun actually accomplished. No, she was not able to stop the war. However, she revealed a crime, a plot to start and legitimize a war. There is no question that had the UN Security Council adopted a proposed resolution to legalize the war, the Iraq narrative would have been different. The invading coalition would have had legal justification for its action. While criticism certainly would have followed mili-tary action, it would have been considered and voiced differently – seen as a coalition of countries, authorized by the Council and acting legally and legitimately. Without Katharine's act of conscience, the invaders would have achieved what they so sorely sought: approval for a horrific, wrongful act.

There exists a compelling and excruciatingly obvious lesson in a time when the 'Iran issue' and Middle East destabilization are of such concern: The Iraq Inquiry Report should be required study for every US and UK lawmaker. Further, it should be first on the international reading list of anyone involved in decision-making affecting Iran and the Middle East. An addition to the study curriculum could well be the writings of Gordon Brown, Blair's successor and Chancellor of the Exchequer at the time Bush and Blair were planning their invasion.

'War could not be justified as a last resort and invasion cannot now be seen as a proportionate response,' Brown writes in 2017.[2]

On numerous occasions, both publicly and privately, Katharine has insisted that she still has no regrets about violating the Official Secrets Act in an effort to stop the war and save lives. 'I would do it again,' she says, words once bannered across newspapers around the world (except in the United States) and accompanied by the photo of a triumphant, smiling young woman. She said it again when she and her infant daughter travelled to Washington DC, where an American University symposium featured Katharine's story and the first edition of this book.

By then, Katharine was in her early thirties and five years had passed since her arrest. She was happily married to Yasar Gun, a Turkish national, and had fallen back on teaching Chinese to British students. Her parents were close by, and they remained proud, dedicated advocates, championing their daughter throughout her ordeal and beyond. Katharine's life was before her, but that single decision – as right as it was for her – would play a major role in her family's future. Most difficult would be finding satisfying long-term employment. It's just not easy when you've been the star of a story like this.

After a while, she and Yasar took trips to his beloved Turkey to explore the possibilities of moving permanently. Making a decision to settle abroad would be difficult for Katharine, despite the challenges she faced in her home country. But finally, in the spring of 2011, Katharine wrote, 'We finally decided to take the plunge.' Since relocating to Turkey, the family has visited England several times, and in 2016, the death of Katharine's beloved mother, Jan Harwood, took Katharine back for a stay with her grieving father.

In her most recent letter, Katharine writes: 'We moved to a

village and live on a farmyard. Our daughter has loved living here; she helps to look after the chickens, goats, sheep, and cows. She wanders off into the fields on her own. There are acres of wheat fields behind the house. She sits and sings songs to herself or writes poetry or draws, she jumps in the haystacks and takes photos of everything, sometimes making videos and introducing the animals. It's a very simple life, and our home has been very basic.'

This author has lived in the countryside of South Dakota for years, and surely can appreciate the attraction of a simple life, the joys of solitude, and the freedom of children playing in nature. However, one also wonders: what have we all lost, with Katharine Gun removed from the dialogue of conscience? Her sharp mind and strong will are exactly what today's political and governmental discussions sorely need. One should never say that because Katharine is intelligent, strong, and experienced that she *should* leap back into the fray – but wouldn't we all be better for it?

Reflecting on her act of conscience and its impact, Katharine's letter concludes, 'I hope my example will give others courage to stand firm against abuse of power and deception.' As for the war?

'In truth, it was a war crime, an illegal war, a war against humanity.'

– Marcia Mitchell, 20 February 2019

THE KOZA MEMO

To: [Recipients withheld]
From: FRANK KOZA, Def Chief of Staff (Regional Targets)
CIV/NSA Sent on Jan 31 2003 0:16
Subject: Reflections of Iraq Debate/Votes at UN–RT Actions
+ Potential for Related Contributions
Importance: HIGH
Top Secret//COMINT//X1

All,
As you've likely heard by now, the Agency is mounting a surge
particularly directed at the UN Security Council (UNSC)
members (minus US and GBR of course) for insights as to
how [to] membership is reacting to the on-going debate RE:
Iraq, plans to vote on any related resolutions, what related
policies/negotiating positions they may be considering, alli-
ances/dependencies, etc – the whole gamut of information that
could give US policymakers an edge in obtaining results
favorable to US goals or to head off surprises. In RT, that means
a QRC surge effort to revive/create efforts against UNSC
members Angola, Cameroon, Chile, Bulgaria and Guinea, as
well as extra focus on Pakistan UN matters.

  We've also asked ALL RT topi's to emphasize and make sure
they pay attention to existing non-UNSC member UN-related
and domestic comms for anything useful related to the UNSC
deliberations/debates/votes. We have a lot of special UN-related

diplomatic coverage (various UN delegations) from countries not sitting on the UNSC right now that could contribute related perspectives/insights/whatever. We recognize that we can't afford to ignore this possible source.

We'd appreciate your support in getting the word to your analysts who might have similar, more in-direct access to valuable information from accesses in your product lines. I suspect that you'll be hearing more along these lines in formal channels – especially as this effort will probably peak (at least for this specific focus) in the middle of next week, following the SecState's presentation to the UNSC.

Thanks for your help.[1]

PART I

INVITATION TO A CONSPIRACY

CHAPTER 1: Message Sent

To: [Recipients withheld]
From: FRANK KOZA, Def Chief of Staff (Regional Targets)
CIV/NSA Sent on Jan 31 2003 0:16
Subject: Reflections of Iraq Debate/Votes at UN–RT Actions
+ Potential for Related Contributions
Importance. HIGH
Top Secret//COMINT//X1

All,
As you've likely heard by now, the Agency is mounting a surge particularly directed at the UN Security Council (UNSC) members (minus US and GBR of course) for insights as to how [to] membership is reacting to the on-going debate RE: Iraq . . .

I T BEGAN IN the wee hours of the morning at the National Security Agency's National Security Operations Center not all that far from Washington, DC, where Frank Koza, chief of the Regional Targets group, sat composing a highly secret message. Aside from the usual Intelspeak, his message was straightforward and to the point. It was addressed to his counterparts at the Government Communications Headquarters (GCHQ) in Cheltenham, England.

Koza's e-mail was very much in keeping with the business

of the NSA, an enterprise little understood by most of the American public, who are much more familiar with the CIA and the FBI, often in the news for questionable management and various commissions and omissions and, less often, for jobs well done. It is the NSA that seems the most obscure, most mysterious of the intelligence agencies.

By design, the NSA remains in the shadows, hidden behind a wall of security in Maryland. Its work is beyond top secret, beyond imagination. A city unto itself, it excludes the outside world and likely could survive comfortably if the rest of civilization vanished in the blink of an eye. It is unbuggable and impenetrable. It stores more secret information than all other hush-hush data collectors combined. Its technical capabilities are mind-boggling and imply that private international communication, by whatever means, is not private at all.

Koza's addressee is similarly not as well known worldwide as its more glamorous sister agencies, MI5 and MI6, popularized by British fiction. GCHQ is infinitely more secret, with far greater resources than its intelligence siblings. To those knowledgeable about intelligence matters, GCHQ has an impressive significance by virtue of inheritance. Its predecessor was the historic Government Codes and Cypher School at Bletchley Park, where the British broke the infamous German Enigma code during World War II. Now, five thousand staff on the GCHQ payroll speak and listen in 107 different languages every hour of every day. This morning, thousands of miles from Koza's desk, one of them, Katharine Gun, would be reading in English.

Coincidentally, this same day, 31 January 2003, the British foreign secretary, Jack Straw, announced the selection of GCHQ veteran David Pepper to replace Sir Francis Richards as director of the agency. Pepper, with an impressive intelligence background, would assume his new position in April, just in time to inherit the Koza problem.

Also on this same day, then US national security adviser

Condoleezza Rice would attend a highly secret and decidedly bizarre meeting in the Oval Office with George W. Bush and Tony Blair, where the topic of conversation would have much to do with what was now taking place at the NSA.

More than one reliable source concludes that the message from Koza was Rice's inspiration. However, a former NSA officer puts his money on Vice President Dick Cheney, for whom desired ends and means for getting there are sometimes considered to be in conflict with the law. The view of unnamed US intelligence officers suggests a team inspiration from Rice and Donald Rumsfeld, along with George Tenet, then CIA chief, and USAF Gen. Michael Hayden, then NSA chief.

Seen as directly complicit in the 31 January fiasco, Hayden has been alleged in the past to be somewhat careless about complying with various laws governing surveillance of individuals. It is true that the four-star general has fiercely disputed such allegations. He has described the NSA's lawyers as being careful about ensuring the lawfulness of the agency's actions 'out of a heartfelt, principled view that NSA operations had to be consistent with bedrock legal protections'.[1] And, later, that 'Everything that the agency has done has been lawful.'[2]

That seems not to have been the case on 31 January 2003.

Hayden, who has spoken so definitively in defending the NSA's compliance with the law, has spoken with equal conviction about other aspects of the secrecy business. One statement in particular, uniquely related to this story, seems especially disconcerting: 'I'm not too uncomfortable with a society that makes its bogeymen secrecy and power . . . making secrecy and power the bogeymen of political culture, that's not a bad society.'[3]

In the end, Frank Koza's message sent from the agency headed by Hayden was all about secrecy and power, about using illegal means to gain power over a small group of suddenly important individuals and nations.

This very day a bogeyman, a monstrous American bogeyman, was about to saunter into Katharine Gun's office and fire up her computer screen. The question was, what to do with him?

CHAPTER 2: Message Received

At the time, it seemed to me that if people knew how desperate
Bush and Blair were to have a legitimate reason to go to war,
our eyes would be opened . . . people would see that their
intention was not to disarm Saddam, but in fact to go to war.
                                                    – Katharine Gun, April 2005

'IT WAS QUITE cold that Friday morning of 31 January
    when I woke up about nine o'clock beside Yasar, still
    sleeping. At GCHQ we had flexible hours, and my
workday usually began at about ten o'clock and ended after
six, so sleeping until nine was not unusual. Our bedroom was
light and bright with natural wood floors and white walls, with
cream-coloured curtains. It was a cheerful place to begin the
day, even on a cold winter morning – not like the rest of the
house, a dreary place with small windows. I got up, pulled on
jeans and a T-shirt, and layered on a jumper, because I might
want to walk home after work and it would be cold. I always
dressed casually for work; most people at GCHQ did.[1]

'Yasar drove me to work in our old, beat-up red Rover
Metro. We had a cuddle and kiss before he dropped me off
outside the gates of GCHQ. I waved goodbye and he drove
off to work at the café. Inside, I bought a coffee and a cinnamon
roll at the shop and settled down to work. It was all so normal,

so ordinary. There was nothing to suggest that this day would change my life.

'I went to my desk, finished the last of my coffee, and opened my e-mail. And there it was.

'I could not believe what was on the screen, and I had to read it several times. I felt quite excited – no, more shocked than anything else. And it suddenly became clear to me that this message was so significant that perhaps it could be used to bring a stop to the rush for military action against Iraq. My thoughts were racing, really bizarre thoughts for me. I had never intended to do anything like that which I was now contemplating. I certainly had not been looking around for information to leak. The thought honestly had never occurred to me. But now, the fact that I was a recipient of Koza's request made me feel as if I had moved into a different sphere, as if my life had suddenly taken on new and unfamiliar dimensions. I was, in this new place, privy to the internal workings, the most secret workings of top government – workings that seemed so very wrong.'

On Katharine's screen was a blatant invitation to a conspiracy. The United States was mounting an illegal intelligence operation against the UN Security Council member nations – and their representatives – that would cast the deciding vote on a resolution for war against Iraq. At the moment, the undecided were resisting US pressure for an 'aye' on launching a preemptive strike.

The purpose of the operation was explained – to collect 'the whole gamut of information that could give US policymakers an edge in obtaining results favorable to US goals'. Clearly, the principal goal was war. Sooner rather than later. Called for was listening in on not only office communications, but also 'domestic', private conversations.

Britain was asked to join 'a surge effort . . . against UNSC members Angola, Cameroon, Chile, Bulgaria and Guinea', with special attention on Pakistan. Other UN delegations not sitting on the Security Council at the moment were also good targets because they could 'contribute related perspectives insights whatever.' The message, sent by the NSA's Frank Koza, recognized that 'we can't afford to ignore this possible source'.

As for timing, Koza wrote, 'this effort will probably peak (at least for this specific focus) in the middle of next week, following the SecState's presentation to the UNSC'. It was important to know how the 'swing voters' reacted to Colin Powell's weapons of mass destruction (WMD) pitch to the Security Council and, it seems, to collect secrets that could manipulate those reactions, ensuring that they would be 'favorable to US goals'.

'I sat there, mesmerized, appalled by the fact that the public rhetoric of George Bush and Tony Blair, especially Tony Blair at that time, led us to believe that all efforts were being directed toward securing a diplomatic resolution to the matter of Iraq, not toward an inevitable war. They talked of other options: Saddam Hussein being forced to give up his WMD, or having to leave Iraq. It seemed so hypocritical that they were saying this on the one hand in public, and behind everyone's back, they were desperately trying to seek a yes-vote to the second resolution to justify a war that they obviously wanted. They were willing to use any means to get what they wanted.

'It seemed to me, as I sat there thinking, that if people knew what really was going on, they would understand that the intent all along was war, not disarmament. I asked myself: How could anybody even hope for a chance of resolving the issue peacefully when the motives of the US administration were so apparent, so blatant? Besides, I didn't think that the job of the intelligence services was to manipulate, to politicize intelligence. I don't believe you should tailor intelligence to a political agenda. I was angry – angry about their trying to manipulate the vote in the Security Council.

'I knew there were others like me at GCHQ who were worried about this rush to war, who had serious questions in mind.'

By a strange coincidence, a memorandum had been circulated to staff exactly one week earlier. It read, 'I know from the questions you have asked . . . that some of you have concerns about the legal or ethical basis of war against Iraq – if and when it happens – and GCHQ's part in it.' 'Well,' assured the senior officer responsible for the memorandum, 'there is no question of any member of GCHQ being asked to do anything – at this or any other time – which is not lawful.'

It is likely that the author of the memorandum to staff believed what he wrote so convincingly. Further, he assured, 'British troops do not go into action unless the Attorney General has advised the Prime Minister that their action is lawful.' The directive also quoted the prime minister's remarks from two weeks earlier, when he promised he would never commit British troops to a war he thought was 'wrong or unnecessary'. Besides, the government 'has shown its commitment to trying to resolve this difficult situation by agreement with the international community, through the United Nations'.

Through the United Nations. By doing what the Koza message asked? Creating a false coalition? Would the United Kingdom join the United States in this apparent hypocrisy?

That night, after work, Katharine did not take the bus but instead walked several miles into town through the dark and the cold, wanting to be alone with her thoughts. One in particular, she says, 'was already running around in my head, that this was explosive stuff'. She reached the café shaking with a combination of cold and rattled nerves, pulled off her heavy sweater, and folded into a chair to watch her husband finish his chores before closing. Nothing was said, not a word about the Koza message. He could not know, not at this point. It was a matter she would have to decide for herself, unless, of course, she had already decided. She thinks, perhaps, she had.

'To be honest, I must admit that the decision to leak the e-mail was instantly in my mind as soon as I read it, not finally made, but certainly in my mind. It was there because of the nature of the message and the impact on me.

'At the time, all I could think about was that I knew they were trying really hard to legitimize an invasion, and they were willing to use this new intelligence to coerce, perhaps blackmail delegates, so they could tell the world they had achieved a consensus for war. I felt so strongly, and I knew there was so much public anxiety and anger about a pre-emptive strike, about rushing into war, that I didn't really think about my own personal circumstances at that stage.'

It is along about here in Katharine's story that her critics howl. What did she think the NSA and GCHQ were doing? Knitting sweaters for poor children in third world countries? She was in the spy business, for God's sake, they will say. And what was afoot in the business at the moment was a spy operation. Surreptitiously, clandestinely collecting information. The United States and United Kingdom were simply trying to acquire information about the positions of the various target countries. Nothing new – in fact, so old hat as to be boring. So what, they ask, was her problem about a bit of high-stakes eavesdropping at the United Nations?

'Yes, it was eavesdropping,' Katharine agrees, 'and that's what I did for a living.' But what she did in the normal course of her work was something quite different, as she sees it, from what GCHQ was being asked to do by the NSA. 'This request was far more than attempting to collect information on negotiating patterns, on likely responses to draft proposals.' It was how the information was to be used. Here Katharine and her colleagues were being asked to help manipulate those patterns and responses, to legalize what otherwise might well be an illegal war. Much later, in the spring of 2005, what was going on was described to the public as tailoring intelligence to fit policy.[2]

'You're being asked to participate in an illegal process with the ultimate aim of achieving an invasion in violation of international law,' Katharine says. An illegal process with the imprimatur of a bogeyman on the loose.

Ultimately, Katharine believed that if the Koza message was released to the public, people would see clearly that, despite official government pronouncements about seeking a diplomatic resolution to the Iraq problem, behind-the-scenes unofficial government was in pursuit of quite a different solution. And that solution would allow the United States and United Kingdom governments to claim that a unified United Nations believed Iraq was in contravention of Security Council resolutions and was an imminent threat to world peace. War, then, would be both legal and necessary.

Timing was a significant issue.

'We were all aware that Hans Blix and the WMD inspectors had not yet had a chance to complete their work. From the beginning it had been estimated that it would take them at least six months once in place to provide any kind of realistic assessment. They had been there about three months when Koza's message arrived. This was troubling, I would guess, for a lot of us.'

Yasar worked on Saturdays. For Katharine, this Saturday was a day of moving about in something of a fog, the real world obscured behind a hazy scrim, where the words of the NSA memo were all that seemed clear, spelling out what would happen if she were to reveal its contents.

'At no point during the weekend did I consider telling any of my family members, or even Yasar, because I didn't want to jeopardize anyone else. I wanted everyone else to be wholly innocent of the affair. But also, at the back of my mind, I was thinking that if I did it, I would do it anonymously. And, hopefully, no one would ever know it was me. We regularly see in the press leaks from official sources, and there never seems to be any kind of retribution, anybody being arrested or charged for making those leaks.'

The question that tortured her throughout the weekend was this: Will I get away with it? She felt confident that she would, that she could remain anonymous. Later, she realized that she didn't know how to play the game, didn't know the unwritten rules.

'I knew there are people, especially those who work in London in both the civil service and the intelligence service,

who brief journalists very much below the radar, sort of un-
officially, without jeopardizing their positions. And they get
away with it. You read about the leak, oh, not one of this nature,
but you never hear about who was responsible or a manhunt
under way to find the source. No one is punished. No one is
identified. This is what I hoped for. This is what I expected.'

Looking back, Katharine recognizes the problem. The 'official unofficial' briefings – call them 'controlled leaks' – are for
the most part institutionalized. A selected journalist, one from
each major news entity and each category of news within that
entity, communicates directly with his or her assigned contact
within an intelligence service. There are unwritten ground
rules. The intelligence contact is never named and the information provided is reported to have come from 'known reliable'
or 'unnamed government' sources. The arrangement is mutually
beneficial; journalists get information for their stories, and the
government releases certain information it wishes to get to the
public without having it attributed to a specific individual.
Amateurs like Katharine are not allowed to play the game.

There was a caution that kept returning, a fear that had to
be placed into the emotional conflict of indecision. Or, perhaps
a decision made but not yet wholly accepted. It was the critical matter of Yasar's safety.

They were wildly in love, these two, the blonde, petite
Englishwoman and her 'beautiful, beloved' husband. Just six
months earlier, Katharine had married the man of her dreams,
the tall, dark Mediterranean charmer with finely chiselled
features and a quick, expansive smile. They met at the café
where he worked, where she would go for coffee in the evenings
after leaving GCHQ. He would wink from across the counter,
and she was enchanted. 'He was the most beautiful man I'd
ever seen,' she says.

The café, small, unpretentious, was a comfortable, intimate
place, ideal for chatting after work, when the chat had to be
about anything but work. Filled with light, the café was perfect
for people from GCHQ, whose days were spent in a darkness

that had nothing to do with either natural or artificial illumination.

Most evenings, Katharine was accompanied to the café by a male GCHQ colleague. Yasar, eyeing pretty Katharine seated with her companion, assumed she was 'taken', which was not true. The man with her was a friend, not a boyfriend. Since Yasar made no advance other than a wink now and then, Katharine assumed he was not interested. This, too, was not true. Finally, unaccompanied to the café, Katharine winked back. He came to stand beside her.

'I'm going to the cinema,' she said, and then, surprising them both, 'what are you doing later?' He had a break, he told her. Would she like to go for a walk? Yes, she would very much like that; she had time for a walk before the picture started. From that moment on, Katharine Harwood had no space in her life for any other man. Winking led to frequent evening walks, which eventually led to dating. They were married in an intimate ceremony attended by a small group of friends and her parents, newly arrived from Taiwan. The family met the enigmatic young man for the first time the night before the wedding.

'I felt better after meeting him,' Katharine's father, Paul Harwood, says. 'He obviously adores her.'

Weeks after they first started dating, Katharine discovered that Yasar, still learning English, often communicated with customers in the café by winking. It was a way of greeting people. 'He winked at everyone,' she laughs.

There was little to laugh about when, two weeks after the marriage ceremony, Yasar was picked up by immigration authorities and taken into police custody, where he was held incommunicado until the following morning. Rushed to Heathrow airport, he was prepared for deportation to Turkey. In their home with her family now up in the north of England, Katharine was on her own and near panic. The fear that she would never see her husband again was suffocating.

Katharine made an urgent call to a solicitor, begging, 'Please help us.' They were legally married, she explained. She was a UK citizen! How could this happen? With help, the mess was untangled, government officials called officers at the airport, and the bridegroom was released just moments before the plane bound for Turkey left the gate. A devastatingly close call.

Yasar's visa, extended, was still temporary. He had asked for asylum, given unsettled political issues in Turkey. They were awaiting an answer. Finally, eventually, Katharine put her money – and Yasar's safety – on anonymity. It was an egregiously unfortunate wager.

By the afternoon Katharine had decided to make one call, to tell one person about the Koza message. (She has guarded that person's identity throughout the whole affair.)

'I called the person that I ultimately sent the e-mail to. I haven't named her in public and I won't. Let's just call her Jane. She was the only person I talked to about this, and I could trust her. I knew how she felt about the war, about the impending invasion of Iraq. We both felt pretty much the same way about the whole issue. I also knew that she had been in contact with a member of the media who probably would help. I didn't know anybody else whom I could trust and who had a contact like that. So I called Jane to tell her what I'd seen. I didn't go into details; I just said that I'd received an e-mail I thought was damaging enough that, if it were leaked, might have the effect of preventing the war – or at least delaying it until other options had been exhausted. I asked her if I could send it to her, or perhaps she suggested that I could send it to her.'

On Sunday morning, Katharine and Yasar had a 'lie-in', then a big Turkish breakfast of olives, cheese from his home country, tomatoes, cucumbers, lots of toast, and a big pot of tea. Together they cleared away the breakfast things, chatted easily, read the voluminous Sunday newspaper. Later they took a ride out into the countryside, stopping at a picturesque little village for afternoon tea. It was all so deceptively normal.

As usual, Yasar fell asleep to soothing music, drifting off long before his wife on Sunday evening. This night, it would take Katharine an uncharacteristically long time to fall asleep, music or no. She was remembering the GCHQ staff memo of one week ago.

'Concerns from a moral or ethical standpoint [regarding war against Iraq] are a personal matter,' it acknowledged. Worries shouldn't be kept to oneself. Anyone having reservations about what they were asked to do should contact the Welfare Office, the staff counsellor, or one of three specifically named senior officers. No, she thought. A slow-moving, red-taped, and supremely protective bureaucracy was not the answer.

Unwritten, but clear in its intent, was a warning to GCHQ staff. And that was what was keeping her awake.

CHAPTER 3: Four Weeks That Changed Everything

More of a concern to us was that we would be joined in the prosecution. To publish is an offence under the Official Secrets Act as well. We were as culpable as Katharine. But they're cowards. So they preferred to take on the little guy – in this case, little woman – rather than us big guys.[1]

– Martin Bright, *Observer* editor

What I hoped was that people would see what was happening and be so disgusted that nobody would support the war in Iraq. And if anybody would go to war it would be the United States going it alone. And I even hoped that the US general public would somehow realize that they were being dragged hook, line, and sinker into the war.

– Katharine Gun, to the authors

AN UNSUSPECTING YASAR drove his wife to work on Monday morning, stopping at the GCHQ gate long enough to give her a quick squeeze and a kiss before reaching across to open the passenger door for her. She gave him a smile, climbed out of the car, and stood watching until the red Metro was out of sight. As she turned to enter her secret world, she felt transparent, as if everyone around her would see through her and into her. Would see the pounding heart and knotting stomach. Would see into her mind and be appalled by the conspiracy of her thoughts.

The final decision to act had been made. When? She wasn't certain. Possibly in those first few minutes on Friday, when Koza's message appeared on her screen. Perhaps during the solitude of her walk to the café to meet Yasar after work, or while talking with Jane later. At some point, there was no emotional turning back. More likely, it had been there, the *finality* of it, after her talk with Jane.

'This morning, Monday, I worked in a different office from the one I normally worked in, so I thought it would probably be a good idea to print a copy off from that computer, rather than the one that was my normal terminal. Obviously, this is all an indication of how I was trying to remain as anonymous as possible. I brought up the e-mail, looked at it one more time, then copied it and pasted it to a different window. I printed it off and put it in my handbag. Of course, if I were caught, that's where anyone would look, wouldn't they?

'I was planning to take the e-mail outside GCHQ's grounds, which is already breaking the law, regardless of whether or not you make it public. You weren't, without prior permission, permitted to take classified documents off GCHQ territory. I knew exactly what I was doing.'

Up to this point, it is true that Katharine had broken no law. Once she removed the copied document from the premises, which she fully intended to do, she could be charged with high crime against her country. The thought made her ill, and throughout the day she reminded herself that this was something right, that she was not a criminal. What she was doing, however, identified her as precisely that.

'I guess some people would accuse me of being naïve, in that I didn't consider the ramifications of what this act would be for me personally. And that's probably true, in the sense that I've never done anything really bad. I mean, I had never done anything that could be considered a crime. It made it very difficult to consider what I was doing as a criminal offence. In fact, it felt like it was the only morally right thing to do. Oh, I was of course frightened and nervous, but – and it's hard to explain – I didn't feel frightened or torn apart by my decision, once it was made.

'So, call me naïve if you will, but obviously if I'd been selling state secrets to somebody considered to be an enemy, an arch-rival, that would be a totally different issue. If I had been leaking information not in an attempt to prevent unnecessary loss of life, that would have been different. There are degrees of breaches of official secrecy, and I didn't feel that mine was a criminal offence. I believed I was doing the right thing.'

The following day Katharine posted Koza's message to Jane. When it arrived, Jane read the words that had so distressed Katharine and decided to pass it along as agreed. Had she known what was to come later, Jane might well have destroyed the message the minute it reached her. But she did not know, and she felt confident that her friend Katharine would not betray her, that she would not be considered a co-conspirator.

By that Monday morning when Katharine was printing Koza's message, other recipients were responding in quite a different way. It is assumed that Sir Francis, in his last two months as the head of GCHQ, responded both favourably and immediately, authorizing cooperation with the NSA. According to sources close to the intelligence services, the US request for UK cooperation was indeed 'acted on' by the British.[2]

At the time Koza's request arrived in the United Kingdom, there were at least some intelligence and other government officials asking critical questions, secretly of course, about the legality of an invasion. The whole business was sticky, and it seemed fairly obvious that the United States was asking for help not only with electronic black bagging, but also with what could become high-stakes political blackmailing.

At the very highest level, it already was known – and had

been since April 2002, when Blair and Bush met in Crawford, Texas, and reached an accord for military action – that the rhetoric coming from the White House and Downing Street was only that.[3] The decision to invade Iraq had been made, pushed by George Bush and his neoconservative team. It was now essential to find an excuse, an acceptable rationale for doing so. Twisting the arms of the recalcitrant UNSC representatives in order to win approval for a new resolution could supply a universally acceptable rationale. If regime change came about as a result of invasion based on a WMD threat, well, that would be serendipity within the rules. Thus in some lofty quarters, where the strategy was either known for certain or even 'twigged', there was neither shock nor surprise when the Koza message arrived at GCHQ.

'For four weeks I was nervous, on edge. Every day I frantically searched the papers and watched the news. I figured it would take a few days to appear, but then, day after day, there was nothing. It was difficult trying to live normally, as if nothing had happened. It was a struggle, I mean, going about life that way. Everything was quiet, for those four weeks, and I began to think that perhaps it wasn't actually of interest to anybody. Perhaps it would never be made public. I suppose I was a little bit relieved. I could go on with my life as before, and everything would be the same.

'No one would know what I had done.'

The news that Katharine was reading during this period showed an intense ratcheting up of the pitch for war. Three days after she posted her letter to Jane, Colin Powell went before the United Nations – and the world – to explain why war was absolutely necessary, that Saddam Hussein had stockpiles of weapons of mass destruction ready to destroy his neighbours and threaten the peace and security of everyone everywhere. Details about the kind and numbers of weapons known to be in Iraq's possession were supplied. And he was convincing, this highly respected member of the Bush administration. Handsome, charismatic, articulate, respected – no one else in the Bush administration could have done the job so masterfully.

In New York, among the many secret meetings going on with members of the UN Security Council that were of particular interest to Washington were those led by Chile's Juan Gabriel Valdés and Mexico's Adolfo Aguilar Zinser. The two were continuing the fight against a resolution definitively authorizing use of military force against Iraq. Both men were highly respected diplomats, and their colleagues were listening to their concerns.

Aguilar Zinser was particularly annoying to the United States during these intense four weeks. A lawyer and former senator, he dissected the Bush–Blair draft resolution line by line. He complained about what he believed to be obvious conflicts with international law. He threatened to 'throw the book' at both countries. Colin Powell met with Aguilar Zinser and reportedly shook his finger at him, 'jokingly' scolding him for troublemaking.

The uncooperative and obstructionist behaviour of both Valdés and Aguilar Zinser led to repeated efforts to get the diplomats replaced in their roles at the United Nations. But the anti-war heads of state in both Chile and Mexico were refusing to capitulate during this crucial period of negotiation. In Mexico, President Vincente Fox was clearly gaining prestige for refusing to respond to American pressure. Said one Mexican diplomat at the time, 'The Americans don't understand. The more they ask for his [Aguilar Zinser's] resignation, the more they are hammering him into his seat.'[4] Later, the two UN diplomats would reap unfortunate rewards for their efforts, as both Chile and Mexico – bruised by White House cold shouldering – would finally give in to US demands.

Independent journalist Yvonne Ridley was sending news reports from Afghanistan following the US/UK invasion when she was captured by the Taliban, treated unexpectedly well, and eventually released. The capture and release brought Ridley a measure of fame she had not enjoyed before her unplanned adventure. At the time Jane's message reached her, the journalist was travelling the United Kingdom on a lecture tour. Her subject was more than Afghanistan; it was her conversion.

During captivity, Yvonne became interested in Islam. Upon her return to England, she made the decision to convert. She also became, in the process, a strong anti-war protester. Yvonne was colourful, certainly controversial, and she had worked for several British newspapers.

Yvonne explained, 'I was handed the document in the upstairs of Patisserie Valerie in Old Compton Street, Soho, by a woman I only knew as Isobel [Katharine's 'Jane'] . . . a name I had given her when we first met at an anti-war meeting in Bristol the previous year. When I looked at the document, I was almost shaking with excitement but tried to remain calm and impassive – as an investigative journalist should – but my stomach was doing turns. Judging from previous intelligence documents I'd encountered, I felt this was the real thing because it looked so ordinary. No red stamp in thirty-point shouting TOP SECRET. It was far more subtle than that. Its real significance was hidden in the rubrics or lettering and numbers which, when translated by an intelligence contact later, revealed the document to be highly classified.[5]

'It was the real thing. I called a former colleague of mine on the *Daily Mirror*. I was crestfallen when, after being badgered by me daily, he said that no one in the newsroom had been able to authenticate it and therefore it could not be used. However, journalist Chris Hughes did return it to me by a high-speed bike through Canary Wharf back to my home in Soho.'

Next, Yvonne did the obvious. She called Martin Bright, the London *Observer*'s home affairs editor. His title seems misleading, as he is an expert in international affairs, human rights, and Islamic issues – in concerns that seem outside the realm of 'home affairs'. Yvonne and Martin were old friends, and over the years, the two journalists had developed a trusting professional relationship. Among the newspapers for which Yvonne once worked was the *Observer*.

She says: 'It might sound pretty naïve, but I really thought this could affect the decision to go to war. If the *Observer* could authenticate the document it would, I imagined, cause a furore across the world through the pages of the media. The news would jolt the United Nations into acting, and the British government might just pull back from the abyss. If all of that happened, I felt the United States would not go into Iraq on its own, that this would have a domino effect, with publication of the story in the *Observer* the start.

'The reason I did not write the story myself was that I had become well known as an anti-war speaker and was one of the founders of the Stop the War movement. I felt if my name were attached to the story, it might have diluted its strength, and so I did something I never thought I would do – I gave up a scoop and the exclusive byline tag for the greater good.' They met at a café in Central London, not far from the Soho flat Yvonne shared with her young daughter, who was with her this day. A number of media colleagues have been critical of Yvonne for leaving her daughter at home while she adventured in Afghanistan, but Martin takes exception to this criticism. He admires Yvonne as a colleague and as a mother. She is not only a reliable journalist, but also a good, decent person.

'Yvonne handed me a scrap of paper, with this memo typewritten on it,' Martin says.[6] 'There were no markings on it at all, no evidence of who sent it or who it had been sent to. My immediate reaction was, "what use is this to anybody? You could have typed this out."'

'No, no. Really, honestly, it's for real,' Yvonne insisted. 'You need to check it out yourself.' She said she did not know the source of the message, and Martin believed her. If Yvonne's anti-war, Islamic stance crossed Martin's mind it did so quickly and did nothing to shake his trust in the woman beside him.

Yvonne had written on the back of the paper some identifying marks from the memo's header. They included Frank Koza's name and organization.

Back at the *Observer*, a vetting process began. It was vital to prove Frank Koza and his message were real. Quiet contacts made with intelligence sources led to some amazing responses, the first being that the memo was a likely forgery. There were cautions expressed about the infamous Hitler Diaries, all forgeries. One had to be careful. Most interesting was word from one source within the intelligence community that a renegade operation within MI6 was leaking the message to discredit the government. The idea seemed to have legs.

'We became, at the time, convinced that there were elements within the intelligence service that were so unhappy with the war that they would do this,' Bright says. 'We thought renegade elements against the war had managed to receive this leak through contacts at GCHQ and thought, "One way of stopping this war is to get this out."' Eventually, the journalists believed differently, but for a time, the argument held and the newspaper team moved ahead carefully.

'When you're dealing with areas of intelligence, you are constantly in a strange world,' Bright says, a world in which manipulation of the media by sources is always possible. By now, *Observer* colleagues Ed Vulliamy in New York and Peter Beaumont, also in London, joined Martin. Both, Martin says, 'are older and more experienced'.

Ed, from New York, made the call to Frank Koza at the NSA in Maryland. To his amazement, a switchboard operator responded to his request for Koza's office and immediately put him through to a receptionist. According to Bright, the conversation went like this:

'Frank Koza's office.'

'May I speak to Frank Koza, please.'

'Who may I say is calling?'

'Ed Vulliamy of the *Observer* newspaper in London.' Pause.

'Who do you want to speak to?' the receptionist asked.

'Frank Koza.'

'Sorry, I've never heard of him.'

The *Observer* team now believed they were on solid ground. Ed was asked to check around with various insider sources and learned that the style and content of the message seemed consistent with authentic communications of this nature. They decided, after three weeks of investigation, that the memo was not a forgery, that there was no way it 'could have been set up'.

One final concern was the possibility of legal action against the newspaper.

'More of a concern to us was that we would be joined in the prosecution,' Martin explains. 'To publish is an offence under the Official Secrets Act. We were as culpable as Katharine. But they're cowards. So, they preferred to take on the little guy – in this case, little woman – rather than us big guys.'

The editorial team had to be careful in speaking to sources about the NSA message. Loose talk could lead to a legal injunction prohibiting publication. Earlier, the newspaper had been successful in fighting an injunction in the case of former MI5 officer David Shayler, also charged with violation of the Official Secrets Act. The court's decision had been close, but the *Observer* had prevailed. Bright and company were counting on the government's not coming after them again. The Shayler case had become so high profile that it now stood as a principle against the police going to journalists for evidence. The Shayler injunction application had asked for all meeting notes and tape recordings concerning the case, a broad 'trolling' request eventually denied. Bright notes that a different decision would have meant that every time a journalist wrote about an investigation, an application could be made to 'turn over everything that might be of interest' to law enforcement.

Going on the experience with Shayler, trusting their gut feelings about the authenticity of the Koza message, and figuring that the government would not prosecute the *Observer* for an Official Secrets Act violation, the decision was made to publish three weeks after Bright and Ridley met in Central London.

It was still a risk.

In Washington, last-minute preparations for Powell's historic and, as it would turn out, inaccurate report to the United Nations must surely have been aided by the information requested by Frank Koza and eagerly scrutinized by the folks behind the operation. It was advantageous to know what the opposition was thinking.

The operation continued beyond Powell's performance. For four weeks, the surveillance 'surge' went according to plan. Despite the continuing problem with Aguilar Zinser and Valdés, there was hope in Washington that the swing voters would soon join the right team (if need be, through coercion), that China would hold to its position of abstaining, and that Russia and France could be convinced to go along. In that case, success was at least within the realm of reasonable possibility. It was, until travel along the secret road to war encountered a dangerous, and unanticipated, barrier.

And in Cheltenham: 'I went to my local shop, as usual, on a Sunday morning to get my copy of the newspaper. It was 2 March. I was completely, totally bowled over – gobsmacked – when I saw what was on the front page. It knocked me for six, and I think that's the point where it hit me that I was in trouble. Serious trouble.'

'The United States is conducting a secret "dirty tricks" campaign against UN Security Council delegations in New York as part of the battle to win votes in favour of war against Iraq,' Martin Bright, Ed Vulliamy, and Peter Beaumont wrote. 'Details of the aggressive surveillance operation, which involves interception of the home and office telephones and the e-mails of UN delegates in New York, are revealed in a document leaked to the *Observer*.

'The memo describes orders to staff . . . whose work is clouded in secrecy, to step up its surveillance operations . . .

to provide up-to-the minute intelligence for Bush officials.'

Made clear in both the news story and the memo itself was that UNSC members not specifically named by Frank Koza also were of interest. These would include Russia, France, China, and Mexico. And it would be more than a year later when the full extent of the surveillance was known.

The *Observer* scoop noted that the disclosure came 'amid increasingly threatening noises from the United States towards undecided countries of the Security Council who have been warned of the unpleasant economic consequences of standing up to the United States'. Attributed to Washington sources was information that President Bush's national security adviser, Condoleezza Rice, requested the spy operation. It was predicted, albeit wrongly, that this NSA misadventure would be 'deeply embarrassing to the Americans'.

The nature and depth of news coverage made it clear that this was not going to be one of the usual 'reliable government source' leaks. It was explosive, and there would be demands for accountability. Katharine made her way home in struggling slow motion, manoeuvring through a slog of sickening fear, apprehension, and guilt – guilt only so far as Yasar and her family were concerned. The full realization of what her action could mean to her husband's safety struck her as solidly as a slap on the face. And there were her beloved parents and brother living and working in Taiwan, not to mention Gran in Yorkshire. All those who loved and trusted her.

It was not known who leaked the message or where that person worked. But the fact that the message had been repli-cated in the newspaper, not just its contents reported in an article, that it had been headlined on page one, signalled that naming the betrayer would be only a matter of time. Gobsmacked.

Katharine fell into the house and into Yasar's arms, sobbing, so distraught that he was terrified and had difficulty making sense of what she was trying to say. Katharine handed him the newspaper. 'It was me,' she said. Slowly he read the headlines and the beginning of Bright's story. His reaction was gentle, surprisingly so for a passionate Mediterranean temperament. 'I understand,' he told her. 'You did what you had to do. I am proud of you.'

Yasar tried to comfort his wife, but she could not stop crying. He told her, 'You don't have to tell anybody. Nobody knows it's you if you don't confess. They can't prove anything.'

The fear made her physically ill all that Sunday and throughout the night. Vomiting and diarrhoea left her weak, and she was barely able to dress for work in the morning. She thought about calling in sick but then thought better of it, not wanting to call undue attention to herself. This morning, when Yasar dropped her at the gate he held her close longer than usual, smoothed her hair, kissed her gently. 'I am proud of you,' he told her again when at last she pulled away from him. 'Very, very proud.'

The manhunt was immediate, thorough, and tough. There would be no anonymous source; the source would be found and punished. Too much was at stake at the moment, principally the hotly debated US/UK draft resolution designed to legiti-mize a pre-emptive strike on Iraq and to build a broad-based supporting coalition. Throughout the day, various people were called in for interrogation; wide-eyed and apprehensive, they disappeared and, damp-browed and silent, they returned. The air was thick with fear and suspicion.

Katharine's turn came on Tuesday. She had slept a little on Monday night, but not for long and certainly not peacefully. Her answer to the principal question was simple, direct, and patently false. 'I read the message and I deleted it.' The questioning session was just what she expected. She was well prepared and apparently convincing. Katharine remained outwardly calm during her interview but was mentally awash and weak-kneed when she returned to her desk, unable to focus. Blurred images floated mystically across her computer screen, refusing to settle into place, defying her ability to translate. Somehow, she got through the day. The night would be worse.

Yvonne, in Bahrain, was relieved to see the story published 'after three nail-biting weeks'. Feelings of relief did not last and she feared she would be arrested. She debated whether she should go to Jordan, or even into Iraq.

'Anything,' she says, 'seemed preferable to being arrested.'

CHAPTER 4: Conscience Meets Inspector Tintin

The *Observer* said yesterday that the memo had been leaked to it 'by British security sources who objected to being asked to aid the American operation' . . . a 28-year-old woman employee at GCHQ was arrested.

  – Jeevan Vasagar and Richard Norton-Taylor, *Guardian*

I'm pretty rubbish at telling lies, and I try to be an honest person. If I had continued to lie, I would have been dishonest, like them. I have to say that I've only ever followed my conscience. And it, my conscience, is such a nuisance.

  – Katharine Gun, to the authors

KATHARINE'S NUISANCE OF a conscience would not let her sleep after telling government interrogators on Tuesday that she had read and immediately deleted Frank Koza's message, that she had assumed it had nothing to do with her. The magnitude of the lie was too great, the sense of guilt too strong. Her conscience had made her physically ill, and she reached the only decision possible. After a fretful, sleepless night, and tortured indecision, she determined she would admit to her crime. All hopes of anonymity had evaporated.

On Wednesday morning, Yasar did not drive directly to GCHQ; instead, in silence, he drove aimlessly around the city, delaying the moment when he would leave his wife at the GCHQ gate. She sat at his left, exhausted, head tilted back against the seat, numbed. A tape of Turkish music played softly. There was an amazing sense of serenity in the car.

Wednesday morning was chilly but lovely. The rush hour, such as it was, had passed in this city, a uniquely inviting place resting peacefully on the western edge of the lush Cotswolds. In the distance are ancient forests and gentle hills, a verdant green that extends down to gardens throughout the city. In spite of a modern mall downtown, Cheltenham is typically picture-perfect English, with its elegant Georgian architecture and palpable aura of the past. Here, one can reach out and touch the Middle Ages, can marvel at historic Regency influence.

Although she was raised in Taiwan, Katharine is fiercely, loyally British. She never felt her nationality, her fealty to birthplace, more vibrantly than this day when she knew she was taking the risk of being called 'traitor'.

Finally, reluctantly, Yasar pulled to a stop at the sprawling secret complex located in a suburban setting that seems so inappropriate. But then, that seems to be the way of some of the world's most secret enterprises, settling themselves as they do in bucolic rural or suburban neighbourhoods. Even if the mission is markedly different, one expects a place more ominous; for example, more like Russia's infamous Lubyanka, standing meanly in the heart of bustling Moscow.

Not yet ready for occupancy this Wednesday was GCHQ's new 'doughnut', a circular answer to its five-sided American counterpart in Arlington, Virginia. The new facility is located in the open, where from a short distance away one can stop and gawk at the hub of the United Kingdom's most secret business. This morning, during the drive around Cheltenham, Katharine was thinking that she would not be with her colleagues when it came time to move to the posh new building.

Yasar both knew and understood what his wife had decided, that Katharine had to do what she firmly believed was right, a belief consistent with Yasar's own philosophy of the human experience. This, in spite of his having told her that 'no one could prove anything' if she did not confess. Those were throwaway words, which they both recognized as soon as they were spoken.

The goodbye kiss and cuddle were brief, and Katharine did not look back as the Metro drove away. She knew the scene at the gate would never be repeated.

No coffee, no cinnamon roll this morning. As she entered the office, Katharine, in obvious distress, caught the attention of her manager. Concerned that the young translator was ill, she took Katharine into a side office. With no preamble, with no excuse, Katharine said simply, 'The leak was me. I did it.' She burst into tears.

Visibly shocked, disbelieving at first, the woman said nothing but reached out to put an arm around Katharine's shoulder. When Katharine calmed, her manager took her arm and led her directly to the Security Department, her touch gentle, her obvious concern comforting to the frightened younger woman.

The die was cast, and Katharine's promising future evaporated as quickly as if it had been deleted from her computer screen. Zap. Gone. Permanently, irretrievably deleted. There would be no handy 'undo' or 'restore' options.

Questioning began around ten o'clock that morning, Katharine's interrogators GCHQ security personnel. She was comforted by the presence of her manager, who never left her side. They sat circling a round table, questions and answers posed and responded to with quiet civility. Why? Who? When? And, of course, how? It was necessary to make certain that Katharine was indeed responsible for this egregious breach of the Official Secrets Act.

Two years earlier, on 4 January 2001, Katharine Teresa Harwood signed the GCHQ Statement of Written Particulars, required of all new intelligence officers, and she accepted the terms and conditions set out for her job as a Mandarin translator. It included the paragraph below:

34. OFFICIAL SECRETS ACT

GCHQ is one of the UK's intelligence and security services. As an employee you will therefore be subject to the special provisions of Section 1 of the Official Secrets Act 1989. You are required to sign a document on joining and leaving the Department to show that you are aware of the provisions of this section and of the other provisions of the Official Secrets Act which also apply.

Essentially, the Official Secrets Act makes it a criminal offence for all members, or former members, of the security services to disclose official information about their work. The areas covered by the act include releasing information on defence, international relations, security service activities, foreign confidences, and information that might lead to a crime being committed. Katharine's release of the Koza message fit neatly into the specifically named offences.

Thirteen years earlier, almost to the day, a newly revised OSA made not only secret service officers, like Katharine, but also journalists – like Martin, Ed, and Peter at the *Observer* – subject to prosecution if they disclosed information the British government considers damaging to the defence of the country or to its interests abroad.

Katharine's manager escorted her to lunch, then returned with her to the Security Department. She was not left alone at any time. When the Metropolitan Police arrived, they gave Katharine the chilling news that Scotland Yard was coming to make a formal arrest.

'It was then that it really hit me. I had never been in trouble with the law. I had only spoken to police to ask directions, or when I had things stolen from me. I'd always been the victim, not the criminal.'

At some point, her questioners asked Katharine if she wanted to call a lawyer. She answered that she knew of no one to call and was assured that a duty solicitor would be assigned to her in due course. When Scotland Yard officers arrived, Katharine Gun was arrested for violation of the Official Secrets Act, a serious crime with ominous possibilities of punishment. She was terrified.

Katharine speaks highly of the Scotland Yard officers who arrested and interrogated her, as she does of the Cheltenham 'regular police' who held and confined her. The men from the Yard were thorough but kind, one in particular, whom she calls 'Detective Inspector Tintin', after a cartoon French boy who adventures around the world. 'He is a little blond boy with a sticky-uppy flick in his hair,' Katharine says of him. Because of the serious nature of Katharine's crime, Scotland Yard conducted all post-arrest interviews and investigations.

Katharine was taken into police custody in Cheltenham, where she went through a booking process and then was led to the Custody Suite. Her personal belongings were taken from her – her handbag, watch, necklace, and her belt. There was no body search, but a female officer patted her down.

'They were kind about it all,' she says. 'I knew they were just doing their jobs, and I tried to keep that in mind.' This was not difficult to do, given that she had moved to a far distant mental place, one where she did not consider herself a criminal, where she saw herself as quite different from the usual jailhouse residents. She did not belong with the 'addicts, drunks, and prostitutes' who were the 'regular customers' of this place. Her mental and physical selves had separated.

'Custody Suite' was something of a misnomer. It was a single room with a bare cement floor. The bed was a block of cement holding a plastic-covered foam mattress. Next to the bed was a metal toilet without a seat, with no partition of any kind to offer privacy from police officers who opened the door without warning. 'I was afraid I would be caught on the loo,' Katharine says. Dinner that night was fruit juice and biscuits. She could have asked for a bowl of chilli but did not. As it turned out, this would be the menu item for breakfast.

Once the booking process was over, a duty solicitor was called on Katharine's behalf, and she spoke to the woman over the telephone. Next, she was allowed to call her husband.

'I guess we were both in shock at that stage, when we talked on the telephone. He had already come down to the police station, but they wouldn't let him see me. They told him, "Oh well, we're too busy at the moment processing this and that and whatever. Besides, we have to supervise the visit. Try later." He was asking me on the phone if I was all right, and if I needed anything. He said he would keep trying to see me, but he had no idea what time that would be.

'Yasar learned where I was when my manager called him. I had given her his mobile number and she called him almost straight away. From one o'clock until eight, then, he wasn't allowed to see me. He was so worried.'

There would be no more questioning until a search of the Gun home in Cheltenham was completed, which meant not until the next morning. Yasar told Katharine that night that he found the search terribly upsetting. He had let the officers in the front door, then left the premises. Every inch of the place was searched, and only incidentals taken. These included two books in Turkish from among the dozens of books in the house. Curious, one might observe, that the searchers recognized and confiscated the Turkish texts.

'As to what they were looking for, I think they were just trying to see if there was anything at all that would suggest a pattern of activity. I mean, they didn't need evidence because I had already admitted that I had done it. They took my passport, my mobile phone. I didn't have a computer at the time; they surely would have taken it if I had.

'Later, everything was more or less back in the same position after the search, but you just knew things had been touched. I felt bad, because the house was a rented accommodation,

rented from someone at GCHQ posted to London. I felt bad
that it was his house being searched as well as our dwelling. I
wanted to move after the search, but we continued to live there
for over a year. The owner was very calm and dignified about
it all. He didn't say, as he could have, "How dare you get
yourself in trouble while living in my property?" I think GCHQ
had got in touch with him and alerted him to the search before
it happened.'

Yasar would not sleep in the house the night of the search.
It was eerie, being there, and he went to stay with a friend.

Sometime after eight o'clock Yasar was finally allowed to
see Katharine. They met in a special visiting room, one where
the prisoner enters one side of the room and the visitor the
other. A glass partition in the centre separates criminal and
visitor.

'Yasar cried the minute he saw me. I would have cried
if he had not, but the minute I saw him crying, I thought
no, I've got to be strong. So I was saying, "Look, it's going
to be okay, don't worry. I'll be out tomorrow. Please don't
cry." He brought me comfortable sweat pants and a jacket
to keep me warm. There was only a thin brown blanket on
the bed. He brought some books, but they wouldn't let him
give them to me. Anything he brought in like that had to
be sealed.

'We had only fifteen minutes. But because you can't reach
out and comfort each other, I don't know if more time would
be beneficial. You feel really helpless like that.

'It was such a shock for Yasar. He married a nice, white,
middle-class English girl, who had a nice, secure, sensible job
with the government. A civil servant, well paid, and then she
goes and lands herself in prison.

'The police were quite considerate that night, as nice as they
could be without jeopardizing their professionalism. They said
to me, if I needed a cup of tea or anything like that, I could
ring the bell.

'The police said if I had trouble sleeping there would be a

duty doctor in later that evening, and I could get a sleeping tablet if I wanted one. I did. I got a headache tablet and a sleeping tablet. I'd never taken a sleeping tablet in my life, so I was quite nervous. It worked a treat, and I didn't wake up feeling groggy or anything. But I was thinking, if I take the tablet, will it knock me out instantly? Do I dare go to the toilet before I sleep? Suppose I end up falling asleep on the toilet? But no, it worked really well. I slept soundly, to my surprise.'

She saw both the solicitor and Tintin the next morning, meeting in a small, windowless interrogation room. Katharine learned the solicitor would be assigned to her only temporarily, until permanent representation could be arranged. She had no idea at the time what extraordinary, world-class representation that would turn out to be. In the meanwhile, it seemed painfully obvious that the duty solicitor was out of her depth in attempting to deal with a case that was far beyond her experience. The court-appointed solicitor was accustomed to working with 'street kids' in trouble. Katharine Gun was something else.

Tintin's questions focused on the why and how of Katharine's crime and on whether she had an accomplice. She explained her motivation, and the Scotland Yard officer seemed to accept what she had to say. Interrogation focusing on the question of an accomplice was another matter and reached a stage where Tintin, certain someone else was involved, pressured Katharine for answers. Fearful of betraying Jane, she began to cry, insisting that, 'All the intentions were mine.' In attempting to protect Jane, she had said at the time of her arrest and until this instant that she acted totally alone, that she had mailed Koza's message directly to the newspaper.

Now, under enormous pressure, she asked Tintin, 'Am I obliged to give a name?' He said no. He did not need a name, certain he would learn by investigating communication records and other avenues just who it was Katharine had contacted the weekend prior to printing out the memo. Katharine believes she somehow let slip enough clues, perhaps through e-mail and telephone contacts, to lead investigators to Jane. 'You just don't know what they're capable of,' she says. 'Experienced criminals do, but not people like me.'

Once the police identified Jane as the likely accomplice, they repeatedly questioned her, searched her home, interviewed her family. She denied everything. Without Katharine's naming her and given Jane's refusal to admit to complicity, she was never indicted; evidence was lacking for a conviction. She was furious with Katharine.

'Jane said, "Oh, Katharine! How could you let your guard down?" She said I should have kept quiet and said "no comment," that what I had done was "un-streetwise". It was a bit of a tricky patch for a while, because Jane thought I had let her down, but now, in spite of it all, we are still friends.'

While in Bahrain, Yvonne Ridley received a couple of alarming text messages saying that Katharine had been arrested and police had 'raided a couple of homes'. Finally, after much deliberation, she abandoned thoughts of hiding out and returned to London.

'Later,' Yvonne says, 'Katharine's solicitor John Wadham said he would act for me as the "third person".[1] He revealed that intelligence authorities had been monitoring my mobile phone and that is how they were able to link me to Katharine via Isobel. He contacted Special Branch and told them if they wanted to interview me, to contact him first. This, at least, would stop the prospect of a dawn swoop on my home.'

As it turned out, Yvonne, unlike Jane, was never questioned. But she did receive another kind of special attention. 'I discovered that what happened earned me a place on an FBI watch list, which means I get questioned about my activities and plans every time I visit America. When I am "randomly selected" at airports, fellow passengers always assume it is because I am a Muslim.'

It was especially ironic that Katharine was incarcerated in the Cheltenham jail and her Turkish husband left outside, when the situation had been reversed less than a year earlier.

For two 'ordinary' young people in love, the Guns had had enough excitement to last a lifetime. Unfortunately, it had only begun.

And Katharine, in the months ahead, would see Inspector Tintin again.

PART II

FALLOUT

CHAPTER 5: Detour on the Secret Road to War

It seemed clear that Bush had made up his mind to take military action . . . But the case was thin. Saddam was not
threatening his neighbours, and his WMD capability was less
than that of Libya, North Korea or Iran.
> — Matthew Rycroft, memo to David Manning,
> 23 July 2002

PUBLICATION OF THE Frank Koza message created an
unexpected detour on the Bush–Blair road map to war.
In truth, there were two maps, one public and one secret,
parallel routes with quite different landmarks along the way. As
was known at the time, the stubborn group of swing nation
UN Security Council members – Angola, Bulgaria, Cameroon,
Chile, Guinea, and Pakistan – along with troublesome sceptics
like France, China, and Russia, were already creating disappointing, highly publicized roadblocks.

A proper trip to Baghdad, charted on the public map, required
the United Nations' authorized support of military force; it
required a broad-based, approving coalition. However, standing
in the way was the uncooperative behaviour of the anti-war
bunch, a collection of mischief-makers waving Caution and

Detour signs. The stalemate led to the cartographers deciding that covert intervention was called for, that it was necessary to switch maps. To purchase clandestine travel insurance, as it were. They would buy it from the NSA.

The next-to-last historic marker on the public map was to have been a new UN Security Council resolution, with the final destination the strike itself. Now, there would be no second resolution. It was necessary to bypass that marker post-haste and travel directly to Baghdad, ignoring the niceties of UN resolutions and world approval.

No magic carpet ride to Persia was planned for this perilous secret trip. No yellow brick road leading to Oz, but rather to a mythical destination at least as imaginatively conceived (a quick, easy, slam dunk of a war), a destination sought by a cast of peculiar and intriguing characters doing business in London, Washington, and Crawford, Texas.

The world had come to know the supposedly legal – if, to some, alarmingly accelerated – trip to Baghdad. But as of 2 March, when the Koza message was revealed, the existence of the secret map was, at least in part, also revealed. The world – at least those who took notice – learned that an ugly, illegal business was being conducted by the Baghdad-bound. While open, above-board debate continued with the swing nations, below-board dirty tricks were being played on them.

Those in the know understood that enticements of various kinds were quietly being offered in exchange for pro-war commitments; they also understood that non-compliance with United States wishes could be unhealthy for smaller nations dependent upon US largesse for certain essential needs. But for others, naïve about the art of bully diplomacy, the Koza revelation was shocking.

It was shocking as well to unsuspecting members of Congress and of Parliament, even to those who understood that spying on the United Nations was nothing new. What was new was an obvious and blatant attempt at manipulation of UN votes. This was a different matter entirely.

Together, the United States and the United Kingdom had been travelling a secret and deliberately deceptive route for at least eleven months before the Koza message was leaked. Alone, America had been following the course for several years, if one includes the team of advisers who had been pushing for an invasion of Iraq since the late 1990s. Now, there was George W. Bush, in whose craw Saddam had been residing since the early 1990s – although not nearly as irritably as in that of Dick Cheney, who had been Secretary of Defense during George H. W. Bush's presidency.

The new vice president was in the game for the first Iraq War. Unfinished business could be troubling to a man like Cheney.

All the way around, for both the jaded and the naïve, there is no question that publication of the NSA message to GCHQ was politically and diplomatically explosive. As for the perpetrators, one can only imagine the reaction of NSA director Michael Hayden when he learned of the *Observer* story, which must have happened before the London ink was dry on page one. For Sir Francis, still at the GCHQ helm, the revelation also must have been a moment of horror, the single bright spot the fact that only a handful of insiders knew at the time whether the British had responded to the US invitation to conspiracy. Worldwide outrage would focus on the chaps across the Atlantic. But Richards, and Pepper to follow, would have their competent hands full at home, not only in finding the detestable culprit who leaked the Koza message, but also in dealing with elements of the UK government who would be asking embarrassing questions. Parliament, unaware of the full extent of Blair's commitments to Bush, clearly would become a horrendous headache.

It would be two years before the world learned additional details about the secret map that had charted the course from the beginning or, indeed, about the lies and deceptions related to its existence.

Volumes have been written about America's run-up to war

in Iraq. It is a sad and tawdry tale, but not one to be repeated in detail here, with all the characters, telephone calls, meetings, and pleadings. Instead, focus is directed toward certain British–US aspects that seem particularly significant to this story. Included is mind-blowing information from a 21 July 2002 UK Cabinet Office briefing paper, and a now-notorious 'Downing Street memorandum' dated two days later, both essential in understanding the context and motivation for a very risky illegal spy operation.

The leaked information helps in understanding why a young woman's effort to avert a war was futile, given the secret war planning already under way. The armoured train had left the station, and there would be no stopping it until it reached its final destination.

It should be noted that publication of these secret documents, two and three years after the war began, received little follow-up attention in the US media. A yawn, a ho-hum view prevailed in the weeks following their disclosure. Enough had been said in print and on broadcasts. After all, everyone knew, or should have known, what the Bush camp was up to when it was spinning the WMD story and hiding its real motive for war; they knew, or should have known, that no one really believed Saddam Hussein had WMD. In fact, a Harris poll challenged that position, noting that the share of Americans who believed Saddam possessed WMD at the time of invasion was on the rise; by February 2005, 50 per cent were believers.[1] Following up on these stories would have been helpful to a public's understanding of the magnitude of the deception involved.

Typical was the opinion expressed on 12 June 2005 by Michael Kinsley, *Los Angeles Times* editorial page editor and columnist, who gave the memo short shrift. Who needed a secret memo to know that war was inevitable, that 'the administration's decision to topple Saddam Hussein by force' was decided by the fall of 2002? Kinsley was off slightly; the decision to invade was made in the spring of 2002.

Katharine Gun will not tell how much she knew of what

was going on in her secret world and has spoken publicly only of her outrage at seeing the Koza message, of understanding its meaning, and of her reaction. It is safe to say, however, that she (otherwise naïve) and many of her fellow intelligence officers troubled about the war were aware of at least some of the truth.

Gobsmacking stuff, as it were.

To begin at the beginning, America's future president was alleged to have referred to Saddam Hussein in the early 1990s as 'the man who tried to get my dad'. Campaigning in 1999, he told his audience that he would 'take out' Saddam. By the time he became president, it is not unreasonable to conclude that some sort of amorphous map leading to Baghdad already existed in the mind of George W. Bush, for whom taking out the Iraqi leader seemed an excellent idea.

A map to Baghdad more exact, more elaborate than Bush's existed in the minds of members of his inner circle, the colourful characters who were on the scene well before Bush took office. In addition to Cheney, they include I. Lewis 'Scooter' Libby, convicted of leaking the identity of CIA agent Valerie Plame. Libby's planned leak was an apparent payback for her diplomat husband's disputing White House claims that Iraq was purchasing yellowcake uranium from Niger. Those who assumed Libby leaked Plame's name on instructions from a get-even Cheney were surprised when Libby corrected the record by identifying his source as George W. Bush, who later commuted Libby's sentence.

Among other members of the hawkish circle were Donald Rumsfeld, Paul Wolfowitz, Richard L. Armitage, Elliott Abrams, Richard Perle, John Bolton, and Florida's governor, Jeb Bush.

All were a part of the Project for a New American Century (PNAC), a right-wing think tank and source of a letter to President Bill Clinton in 1998 demanding military action to remove Saddam Hussein. Signatures on the letter included those of Abrams, Armitage, Perle, Rumsfeld, and Wolfowitz.[2] At the time, Clinton's interest in getting rid of the Iraqi president was mainly expressed in dollars filtered to the opposition in support of efforts to topple Saddam. This was not nearly aggressive enough.

In Great Britain, Tony Blair and Foreign Office officials, noting a September 2000 PNAC document titled 'Rebuilding America's Defenses', and familiar with its origin, worried about a secret US map to Iraq – and to other destinations in the Gulf region. PNAC obviously wanted to get rid of Saddam, by whatever means. Perle, however, has been quoted as saying that Saddam was only the first target – nothing short of 'total war' would do the trick.

'No stages. This is total war. We are fighting a variety of enemies. There are lots of them out there. All this talk about first we are going to do Afghanistan, then we will do Iraq . . . this is entirely the wrong way to go about it. If we just let our vision of the world go forth and we don't try to piece together clever diplomacy, but just wage a total war . . . our children will sing great songs about us years from now.'[3]

Former UK cabinet minister the Honourable Clare Short was one of those in Blair's government who doubted that the future held the promise envisioned by Perle. She was desperately worried about what appeared to be a disastrous policy born in the project, and now PNAC members were among President Bush's closest advisers. America was on the wrong path and attempting to drag the United Kingdom along. It was abusing its power, seeking to dominate, heading for certain downfall.

'This is a mad administration! It's the Roman Empire all over again,' she told the authors. 'It was the world's most powerful empire, and then it crumbled. I think America has gone barmy; it is misusing its power, it's spending too much on arms, making itself hated.'[4] Short quotes polls indicating the extent to which hatred of America has increased worldwide in recent years; most significantly, the Iraq War years.

The outspoken British lawmaker strongly cautioned Blair against 'making serious mistakes', against going along with what appeared to be a frightening Bush-led trip to Baghdad. He told her not to worry; he would not blindly follow the American president – not walk the Bush walk. She should be assured, he said, that Parliament would be kept in the Iraqi loop.

It was not.

Clare Short was not alone. A number of her colleagues believed George Bush to be truly obsessed by the idea of being the war president who would rid the world of Saddam Hussein. They counted on Blair to deal with the obsession, and the prime minister continued to insist that nothing was decided upon, that no agreements had been made about joining the United States in going after Saddam. At the time, there was strong feeling that the Palestine state issue must be settled before Blair even thought about Saddam. Blair said he agreed. Palestine first.

On the weekend of 6 April 2002, Bush and Blair met at the president's ranch in Texas. This is where Blair agreed to go along with a military strike against Iraq for 'the removal of Saddam Hussein's regime followed by elimination of WMD'.[5] Here was the secret, number-one, primary reason for war, a reason later deliberately buried under a ton of frightening WMD rhetoric, and with good reason. Regime change was outlawed by international accords binding both the United States and the United Kingdom.

Publicly, the spin had not been on regime change, but solely on the WMD threat to Iraq's neighbours and to Western interests. Blair was concerned about regime change. There was no certainty that removal of Saddam's regime would necessarily lead to elimination of Iraq's WMD. The British view was that even if getting rid of the Iraqi leader was 'a necessary condition for controlling Iraqi WMD, it is certainly not a sufficient one'.[6]

At Crawford, a nervous Blair had his conditions for UK participation in a war against Iraq: efforts must be made to construct a coalition and to shape public opinion; the Israel–Palestine crisis must be quiescent; and options to eliminate WMD through weapons inspections must be exhausted. He remembered Palestine, as he had promised Short and other members of his cabinet. But at some point along the road to Baghdad, Blair would abandon his conditions.

Spinning half-truths and deceptions would become a part of a major effort to shape public opinion by both Bush and Blair. And not only were their efforts directed to an unsuspecting public – the United States Congress and the British Parliament were blindsided as well.

By this time, the president and his White House advisers – Colin Powell and his team versus Donald Rumsfeld and his – were vigorously and often contentiously debating the How and Why of an Iraqi strike. For Powell, however, the Why was most troubling. It is ironic that it would be his task, a year later, to sell the world a defective Why. A 28 April 2002 *New York Times* story got the When and the How pretty much right. Early in 2003, it said, the United States would launch a full-scale air and ground campaign. At the time of publication, denials came from both military and civilian leaders. There was no timetable, no plan for war. Of course, behind the scenes, Rumsfeld and Gen. Tommy Franks at the Department of Defense were deep into formulating war plans, Powell and company were working on a plan for post-war Iraq at State, and the White House was busily debating how to sell the whole business to a reluctant world.

In May 2002 the United States and Great Britain were secretly and illegally bombing Iraqi targets, engaging in war without a declaration of war. The goal was to weaken Saddam's defences and to provoke a response, thus providing a reason for a full-scale attack. Two months earlier, British foreign officers had advised the Blair government that such raids were illegal. Routine air surveillance and attacks were justified in defending Kurds and Shias; anything more was 'not consistent with UN law'.[7]

Undaunted, the United States and United Kingdom began serious bombing of Iraqi targets, with the British planes dropping as much tonnage as their airborne colleagues. Taunted, an uncooperative Saddam refrained from responding. The attacks continued in the guise of allowable routine operations.

In truth, the air strikes were nothing new. They had been going on for years, even before the Bush presidency, part of Clinton's effort to depose Saddam without going to war.[8] But now, it seems there was a new impetus, a compelling need to elicit an actionable response.

Clearly, the policy was changing.

On 2 June 2002, a West Point audience of young men and women training for the business of war sat quietly listening to the words of their commander in chief, George W. Bush. He was candid, focused. He spoke to his mesmerized audience about the doctrine of pre-emption.

'Our security will require all Americans [to] be ready for pre-emptive action when necessary to defend our liberty and defend our lives.' The United States must strike first against another nation to prevent a potential threat from becoming an actual one, the president explained.

If the president's words fell on receptive ears at West Point, they were not so well received in certain other circles. There was the question of evaluating the level of threat involved, of deciding what was 'potential' and what was 'actual'. Further, the United States had long held the position that it would not strike first. Pre-emption was not only a new ethical and political construct, but also a difficult one for most Americans. Wasn't the country's traditional stand, that of striking only in retaliation or in response to imminent attack, one of the national characteristics that made the United States different? But it was not just Americans who asked questions about what appeared to be a drastic change in policy.

On 3 August, John Bolton, then Undersecretary of State for arms control and international security, told BBC Radio 4's *Today* programme, 'Our policy . . . insists on regime change in Baghdad.' The following day the *Observer* said of Bolton, 'His words sent alarm bells ringing in London.'

Of critical UK concern was the need to establish a legal

justification for war. The Americans might be careless about this sort of thing, but the British were not. There were specific and hardbound conditions for legal UK support of military action. Specifically stated in the 21 July Cabinet Office briefing paper were only three reasons considered lawful for UK participation in pre-emptive military action against Iraq: 'In the right of individual or collective self-defence, if carried out to avert an overwhelming humanitarian catastrophe, or if authorised by the UN Security Council.' It should be noted that Tony Blair had already agreed to go to war for the purpose of removing Saddam Hussein from power, regardless of what was reported on 21 July.

On 23 July, two days after closely guarded distribution of the Cabinet Office briefing paper outlining conditions for military action – which just happened to be newly-wed Katharine Gun's twenty-eighth birthday – a top-secret prime minister's meeting took place. Present, among others, were Attorney General Lord Goldsmith, GCHQ head Sir Francis Richards, and 'C', MI6 head Sir John Dearlove.

Carefully recorded meeting minutes ('the Downing Street memo') would later be leaked, despite a caution: 'This record is extremely sensitive. No further copies should be made.'

Discussed were two broad US military options: a 'generated start' or a 'running start' utilizing only sixty days compared with the ninety required in the slower, generated build-up of forces. Ideally, this second option would be 'initiated by an Iraqi *casus belli*', a provoked justification, or more aptly, an excuse, for military retribution. The British were finding this second option a problem. Engineering a justification could prove to be risky. Most interesting is that Attorney General Goldsmith warned the group, 'The desire for regime change was not a legal basis for military action.'[9]

It seemed clear that Bush had made up his mind to take military action, even if the timing was not yet decided. But the case was thin. Saddam was not threatening his neighbours, and his WMD capability was less than that of Libya, North Korea, or Iran.

Dearlove reported conversations with Washington about Iraq. Bush, he correctly understood, had as his principal goal the removal of Saddam Hussein, which he intended to 'justify by the conjunction of terrorism and WMD'. But, Dearlove realized, 'the facts are being fixed to fit the policy'.[10]

As the British mulled over US plans and their own limitations and capabilities for going to war against Iraq, the bottom line seemed to be a question of whether the benefits of military action would outweigh the obvious risks. Timing was a key concern, not just the time needed to marshal UK resources for armed conflict, but also that necessary for 'shaping public opinion'. The British population was strongly against military action. Even more troubling was just how to go about getting Parliament to support a war it did not want.

On 29 August 2002, MI6 received what would come to be known as the '45-minute threat', a report that came 'third hand through a main well-established source via a second link in the reporting chain and originally an Iraqi military source'. In itself, the origin of the information should have been enough to cause serious doubts about its authenticity. But it did not.

Discussion and debate led to serious concern among senior intelligence officers. One officer e-mailed the Joint Intelligence Committee assessment team saying the claim was 'rather strong since it is based on a single source'. Could a final JIC draft read that intelligence 'suggests' rather than 'shows' the existence of these weapons? Others in the intelligence community were becoming nervous. The source may or may not have been reliable. But Tony Blair wanted to go with the strongest possible wording. Here was a threat the public – and Parliament – could understand. And it was one that could be shared with Bush.

A year later, reliable source allegations surfaced that during this time JIC head John Scarlett had urged a 'hardening' of Iraq WMD reports by requesting that details of already disproved claims be included as if valid. Inspectors are said to have refused the request, saying that to include the false claims in their report would be 'dishonest, deceitful and eventually disastrous'.[11]

On 12 September, President Bush addressed the opening of the UN General Assembly, where he threw the Iraqi gauntlet at the feet of the prestigious international gathering. He challenged the United Nations body to face up to the 'grave and gathering danger' of Iraq – or to become irrelevant. The invitation – or ultimatum, depending upon the receiver – was translated into various languages and was unmistakably clear in all of them.

One week later, continuing the theme discussed at West Point, Bush released his administration's new National Security Strategy. It set out a more militarized policy, which, by now and to no one's surprise, relied on first strikes. The United States would never allow a challenge to its military supremacy. Further, the United States would use its powers, both military and economic, to encourage 'free and open societies', with America defining both 'free' and 'open'.

Abroad, work was under way on the content of what would become Britain's notorious intelligence dossier on Iraq. Dearlove was deeply concerned about including the 45-minute claim. He reportedly told Blair, just days before the prime minister presented the document to Parliament, that 'the case is developmental and the source remains unproven'.

Meanwhile, in the UN Security Council, the temperature of the debate over launching a pre-emptive war against Iraq continued to rise by the day. Mexico's Aguilar Zinser, who was attempting to keep discussions productive, asked MI6 at this time: 'Do you have full proof of the existence of these weapons, at any one of these particular sites that you are referring to?' According to Aguilar Zinser, the answer was direct.

'No, we don't.'[12]

Not entirely coincidentally, at the time Aguilar Zinser was one of America's spy targets.

Tension increased between Downing Street and the intelligence services, while the US team nervously kept its fingers crossed. Battles raged between Blair's press officer, Alistair Campbell, and the head of MI5, Stephen Lander. The issue is said to have been disagreement over presentation of 'straight' rather than 'spiced, or sexed up' intelligence.

On 24 September, the British dossier on Iraq was finally published, with a strongly worded introduction by the prime minister.[13] 'The document discloses that his [Saddam's] military planning allows for some of the WMD to be ready within 45 minutes of an order to use them.'

As it would turn out, of course, the 'sexed up' claim was as unreliable as its original source. It would become, however, a significant selling point for war in Colin Powell's remarkable speech to the United Nations five months later. It was a strong and chilling threat and helped Powell make the case for war.

While Blair was going through a proper British 'rough patch' promoting the idea of war to Parliament and even to some members of his cabinet, Bush was making significant progress in selling the Iraqi WMD threat to Congress. Saddam's WMD were a threat to Middle East stability, American interests, and even world peace.

On 11 October, the United States Congress adopted a joint resolution authorizing use of force against Iraq. Bush asked for a vote before the congressional adjournment in October, 'for the sake of peace, for the sake of freedom for our country'.

For the United States and the United Kingdom, the next step was drafting a new UNSC resolution imposing new arms inspections on Iraq and leaving little doubt as to dire consequences for non-compliance. On 11 November, the UN Security Council, in its 4,644th meeting, found Iraq in 'material breach' of disarmament obligations and offered the country a 'final chance' by complying with its tough new UNSC Resolution 1441.

Some three weeks after adoption of Resolution 1441, weapons inspections resumed in Iraq under the supervision of the International Atomic Energy Agency and UN experts. And a month after its adoption, on the sixty-first anniversary of Japan's attack on Pearl Harbor, Iraq submitted a monumental 12,000-page declaration on its chemical, biological, and nuclear activities, claiming it had no banned weapons. The report was received with enormous scepticism. Saddam was back at his old game of lying.

10 December was International Human Rights Day, celebrated in more than 150 US cities. Demonstrations, rallies, and vigils sent a clear message to the White House. War against Iraq, at least for now, was unacceptable. A popular theme of the public outcry was 'Let the inspectors work.' This sort of unfavourable public display had enervated President Nixon; it seemingly only energized President Bush.

A similar message was sent to Downing Street. The number of protesters was unprecedented. There were additional demonstrations in London. Among those marching for peace at various times were Katharine Gun and friends from the intelligence community, each one looking over their shoulder, worried about being seen in the crowd.

In the final significant scene before the holiday break in Washington, before the president and his close advisers would retreat to Texas, Bush approved the deployment of US troops to the Gulf region. There were arguments among the Bush team as to how and when to send how many troops. Timing was essential. Otherwise, the world would take note that war was imminent. Pundits were estimating that by March more than 200,000 US troops would be on the ground ready for war. They came close. And on 11 January, Tony Blair sent a naval task force to the Gulf. Aboard were 3,000 British marines. Two days later, an incautious Blair said that his country could act against Iraq, in US partnership, without a new UNSC resolution.

On the twenty-eighth of the month, George Bush delivered his State of the Union speech, saying that Saddam was not disarming but deceiving.

Three days after Bush's inflammatory message, increasing top-level concern over wavering UN Security Council support for war sent the NSA's Frank Koza to his computer. It was the same day as the Oval Office meeting of Bush, Blair, and Rice at which the understanding was clear. There was a single option left for legitimizing a pre-emptive strike against Iraq. Self-defence wouldn't work, and it was impossible to identify an overwhelming humanitarian catastrophe, given that none was looming on the relevant landscape. They needed a UNSC resolution.

For most of the world, the Oval Office meeting would be kept secret for three years, until its contents were leaked, little by little at first, and then in full, on 27 March 2006, in a *New York Times* front-page story. Revealed was a memorandum written by David Manning, Tony Blair's chief foreign policy adviser at the time. Manning dutifully summarized the shocking discussion that took place between Bush and Blair. The adviser's notes confirmed what some in the intelligence community strongly suspected was happening behind the scenes, despite both public statements and secret assurances to the contrary. Among the suspicious had been certain members of the staff at Cheltenham, where Katharine worked.

It was made clear in Manning's report that George Bush discussed both legal and illegal means of obtaining an internationally recognized green light, an unqualified 'go' for a pre-emptive attack on Iraq. By far, and patently obviously, the best choice was a new UN Security Council resolution specifically authorizing war, authorization lacking in the existing UNSCR 1441. Tony Blair agreed, noting that a resolution, among its other benefits, 'would give us international cover' – international political PR, as it were. Too, a resolution would be lawful, which appears, from Manning's notes and other UK intelligence documents, to confirm that legal authorization for war seemed far more important to Blair than to Bush. Also essential, although not specifically mentioned in this context, would be its value in building a strong military coalition for war.

Alternatives to UN authorization reportedly suggested by Bush that day seem preposterous in the telling and read like lines in a silly, low-budget film. It might be necessary to paint a plane in UN colours and entice Saddam to fire on it, thus creating a catalyst for war. Or a defector could be found and convinced to speak about the existence of the annoyingly elusive WMDs, an existence both Bush and Blair doubted to a degree. And, last, there was the option of assassinating Saddam. Preposterous, but clues as to why having the NSA illegally spy on the personal lives of certain members of the Security Council must have sounded to Bush like a brilliant idea at the time. It would be instrumental in reaching a desired end, and a way of avoiding messy alternatives.

The key to the ugly NSA gambit, then, was Bush's determination to win a resolution at any cost. He insisted to Blair during the Oval Office meeting, 'The United States would put its full weight behind efforts to get [the desired] resolution and would twist arms and even threaten.' No longer could anyone deny the extent to which the president was willing to go to get what he so desperately wanted.

This was the historic day when Koza e-mailed GCHQ. There was too much at stake, too much water over the proverbial dam, too much invested since George W. Bush took the White House in 2001, too much to be lost since the journey began, to depend upon diplomacy.

All that had taken place thus far, all of their plans, were at stake. Baghdad, destination on the road map to war, a pathway pitted with lies and deception, must be reached at any cost. Given all that had transpired, it is clear why the world's two top power brokers were willing to pursue the risky UN spy operation Katharine Gun revealed.

Five days later, US Secretary of State Colin Powell gave his persuasive presentation – complete with charts and graphs and dire threats – to the United Nations. On a chilly February day to follow, the United Kingdom's Joint Intelligence Committee chairman John Scarlett called upon Leader of the House of Commons Robin Cook at his home at Carlton Gardens. His purpose was to brief Cook on the WMD issue. He explained that the infamous '45-minute' threat referred not to missiles, but to battlefield weapons. Further, even those had been dismantled and were not usable because their parts were stored separately. Cook was outraged.[14]

To no one's surprise, on 24 February, the United States, Great Britain and Spain formally introduced the widely anticipated second resolution to the UN Security Council. It concluded that Iraq had failed to take advantage of the offer provided in Resolution 1441; as a consequence, it was time to authorize the use of military force. And, to no one's surprise, France, Germany, and Russia introduced a counter resolution intensifying weapons inspections and saying, 'there is a real chance for the peaceful settlement of this crisis'. The military option, said the three, should be a last resort. But it was far too late for this sort of thinking.

Thus was the scene set for the 2 March publication of the Koza message and the diplomatic and political outrage to follow. Shortly after the *Observer* story appeared, any second resolution became a matter of history, in spite of last-ditch efforts to gain passage.

On 5 March 2003, British intelligence officer Katharine Gun was arrested at GCHQ and held in custody. Some have credited her for having the key role in the resolution's failure; others have ignored her part in its collapse.

What followed her arrest is also a matter of history.

CHAPTER 6: Outrage

I regret that I cannot agree that it is lawful to use force against Iraq without a second Security Council resolution . . . particularly since an unlawful use of force on such a scale amounts to the crime of aggression; nor can I agree with such action in circumstances which are so detrimental to the international order and the rule of law.

— Elizabeth Wilmshurst, on resigning as a
Foreign Office legal adviser

INTERNATIONAL LAW EXPERT Elizabeth Wilmshurst resigned from her lofty government post two weeks after the Koza message was made public. Her resignation shocked Great Britain in the days and weeks following revelations that the United States and Great Britain were up to dirty tricks in the United Nations Security Council; tricks that torpedoed a new resolution authorizing pre-emptive war against Iraq. It is not argued here that those tricks, played by the Bush administration, single-handedly killed all possibility of UN authorization for war. But the spy operation was, to many, absolutely the most significant factor, the fatal blow. And it had exploded in full view of the world public. The United States had gone too far. It was a case of, 'Well, that does it!'

Rather than the embarrassing spy fiasco, Bush and Blair primarily blamed France, with its UNSC veto power, for shooting down the resolution. President Jacques Chirac had warned that a no vote was all but certain. But Chirac was referring not to any resolution for war, but to the one under consideration with its hurried timetable for action. It was the timing that troubled the French – and the Russians, the Germans, and others – who had serious doubts about WMD intelligence reports, and who wanted alternatives exhausted before an invasion. A victim of spin, Chirac's position was misrepresented by both Bush and Blair, translated to an absolute veto on any military action against Iraq. As for China, there is the Chinese–Iraqi oil relationship that played into choosing sides. China was a major customer of Iraq oil and had a lot to lose should things go wrong at this point.

The spin was effective, even in the United States House of Representatives, which should have known better. As part of a protest against 'our so-called ally', French fries in the House cafeteria were renamed 'freedom fries', a display of silliness in the midst of desperate seriousness. Other eateries around the country followed suit, and it was implied that restaurateurs who continued to serve French fries were unpatriotic. In Reno, Tim Wright and Tommy Cortopassi, co-owners of the Chophouse restaurant, demonstrated their patriotism and annoyance at France by pouring expensive bottles of French wine into the street outside their front door. One news source reported that because a local ordinance prohibits pouring liquids into the gutter, the prominent restaurateurs dumped them into a five-gallon paint bucket.

'It's a strong statement,' wine pourer Wright said.[1]

A more reasonable statement came from House member Jose Serrano of New York. 'Should we ban French wine, Belgian waffles or Russian dressing? If Mexico votes no [against war], should Mexican restaurants also be banned?'

French wine and potato protests were the subject of press and public interest in the days following the revelation that

America's super spy agency had been conducting dirty business at the United Nations. That bit of unpleasantness essentially was ignored.

The fact that the two countries were spying on delegates would have surprised only the most naïve, and those who were about to vote on the new resolution were far from naïve. What was surprising, and damning, was the obvious and arrogant intent to steal the vote, to crush opposition by any means necessary. It was going beyond the carrot-and-stick song and dance to which the target delegations had become uncomfortably accustomed. It was unacceptable.

There were highly publicized reactions to the damaging leak that were more immediate than resignations from high places in the British government. The most vociferous came from Mexico's Aguilar Zinser and Chile's Valdés, colleagues who had led the anti–rush-to-war battle in the Security Council.

Aguilar Zinser made damning allegations about the NSA spy operation. He spoke of secret meetings among the uncommitted delegates where alternatives to the US position were discussed and proposed, 'top secret' meetings. At one, a document was prepared and not yet shared with anyone outside the room. 'We had yet to get our capitols to go along with it – it was at a very early stage. Only the people in the room knew what the document said.

'The meeting was in the evening and they [US officials] called us in the morning before the meeting of the Security Council and they say, "We appreciate you trying to find ideas, but this is not a good idea." I say, "Thanks, that's good to know." We were looking for a compromise and they said, "Do not attempt it."'[2]

At one point, a position worked out in secret was taken to John Negroponte, at the time the United States ambassador to the United Nations. But a copy of the position already lay on his desk.

It had puzzled Aguilar Zinser. Who was talking? Who was listening? Now he had his answer, and he was furious.

Later, when Katharine Gun was named as the intelligence officer responsible for identifying who was listening in on Aguilar Zinser's meetings, the Mexican diplomat paid tribute to her courage and her concern for international law. She had done the right thing.

Letters went from the Mexican government to UK Foreign Secretary Jack Straw asking him to 'clarify whether GCHQ was involved in spying on its UN allies'. The Foreign Office refused to comment on the request.

Juan Gabriel Valdés immediately ordered a sweep of Chile's UN offices in New York. Angrily, he reported finding 'hard evidence of bugging'. Meanwhile, Foreign Minister Soledad Alvear asked Chile's ambassador in London to check out the story. 'We heard the accusation in the media and have instructed our ambassador to London to find out whether the information is correct or not.' Deeply concerned, she also contacted Straw for an explanation.

Sadly, Valdés, a Princeton PhD, one of his country's most illustrious intellectuals and most respected foreign policy experts, now found his opposition to the US position politically dangerous. President Ricardo Lagos, normally deferential to the United States and wanting to cultivate a middle ground in the war debate, was himself in a politically dangerous position. The public who had elected him were overwhelmingly opposed to a rush to war. News about the spy operation caught their immediate attention. And no wonder, given that US intelligence has for years been involved in Chile's domestic affairs, including supporting the coup that replaced the duly elected Salvador Allende government with the dictatorship of Augusto Pinochet.

In response to the uproar, President Lagos had several conversations with Blair. Joining the fray was Mariano Fernandez, the country's ambassador to Britain. Why, Fernandez wondered, was the United States spying on Chile? Relations between the two countries had been favourable since the first Bush. What was wrong with the second?

On the one hand, Lagos needed to please the United States; on the other, he needed to respond to constituent pressure. Furthermore, on the table was the eagerly sought, unsigned bilateral free trade agreement with Washington approved in December 2002. Bush had notified Congress that he would sign the agreement two days before the Koza e-mail was sent. But the promised signing was delayed – perhaps, thought many, because Chile had not bowed to pressure that it support the war resolution.[3] Valdés, therefore, was a serious problem to his president. Sources say that both US ambassador to Chile William Brownfield and Spain's UN ambassador Inocencio Arias had made it known to Lagos that Valdés's stinging oratory against the war was neither productive nor appreciated.

Lagos, nervous now about ratification of the trade agreement, announced that Valdés would be reassigned to Argentina; Heraldo Muñoz would be his replacement, effective 1 June. The agreement was signed on 6 June.

As for Aguilar Zinser, he was becoming a thorn in his president's side. Mexico's outspoken UN representative was doing little to improve the traditionally mercurial United States–Mexico relationship. The White House quit returning President Fox's calls when Mexico would not give a firm yes or no to support of the war, a humiliating snub of monumental proportion. Fox suffered through the period of revelations and recriminations that followed publication of the Koza message and, although reluctantly, supported his old friend Aguilar Zinser. He did so, to one degree or another, until November 2003, when Aguilar Zinser, looking back at Washington's unseemly bully tactics, said the United States treated Mexico like its 'backyard'. It was too much. Fox fired Aguilar Zinser. His telephone calls to the Oval Office were once again returned.

Ironically, two years later United States Secretary of State Condoleezza Rice – identified in the initial *Observer* story and elsewhere as the probable mastermind of the NSA plot[4] – spoke highly of Aguilar Zinser after his death in a car crash. He was, she said at a Florida meeting of the Organization of American States, 'a distinguished ambassador at the UN, a fierce defender of human rights and democracy in the hemisphere . . . His untimely death is a loss for all of us who cherish freedom and a vibrant civil society in the Americas.'[5]

There was a time when Aguilar Zinser's fierceness was more than Rice could cherish.

Fallout from exposure of the NSA operation was widespread. Reaction included Russian claims that it played a role in destabilizing international finances.

'The value of the United States Dollar went haywire on Monday in Mexico, as its economy is widely US-dependent. In Santiago, the price of the Dollar also went up on Monday as markets could play a decisive role in Chile's final decision.'[6]

For the most part, nations affected by the NSA spy operation kept their political mouths shut about their reactions to what happened on 2 March 2003.[7] Reliable sources say that fear of retribution by the United States was – and is – real and profound. On the same day the original *Observer* story appeared, the *Washington Post* wrote about the swing voters, saying that, 'Their indecision is not over war with Iraq; all have indicated dislike of the US measure and prefer a compromise . . . What they remain undecided about is whether to risk opposing the United States.' Especially smaller countries, countries like those who were spied upon.

There were other stories now surfacing that pointed to alleged coercion being applied by the Bush administration. There were reminders of Yemen's vote in opposition of the first Gulf War in 1991. James Baker, Secretary of State at the time, warned Yemen that its vote would be 'the most expensive vote in history'. For Yemen, with much of its US aid cut off three days later, it was exactly that.

Some UN representatives made light of what happened to their missions, which surely must have pleased the United States. 'It [spying] goes with the territory,' said Pakistan's ambassador,

Munir Akram. 'Anyone who thought it wasn't going on is a bit naïve. It is regarded as one of the privileges of the host country.'[8]

Katharine Gun, noting Akram's observation, says, 'It's true. Collecting information from UN delegations has become a surveillance art form. The problem here is how the information was to be used. Collection is one thing. Manipulation, perhaps even blackmail, is another. And this operation targeted not only offices, but also homes, private lives.'

Bulgaria's ambassador Stefan Tavrov was coyly flattered by the NSA attention. Having the United States target his country made it more prestigious in the international arena. 'It's almost an offense if they don't listen,' he observed. 'It's integrated in your thinking and your work.'[9]

On Sunday, 9 March, the *Observer* reported that the United Nations had begun a top-level investigation into the bugging of its delegations by the United States. The night before, sources in the office of UN Secretary General Kofi Annan told the *Observer* that the UN's counterterrorism committee had discussed the gross violation of international accords and would be following up with an investigation. The British article quoted American Daniel Ellsberg, 'the most celebrated whistle blower in recent American history', who leaked the infamous Vietnam War-era Pentagon Papers.

Gun's leak, said Ellsberg, was 'more timely and potentially more important than the Pentagon Papers'. Mainline US press, in its determination to avoid the NSA story, chose not to carry his comments. Much later, in speaking with the authors, Ellsberg reiterated his assessment of the value of Gun's leak.

International attention was quickly directed toward the NSA and how it collected its information. There was speculation that the West's super eye in the sky, Echelon, was the culprit. Two days after the UN spy operation was made public, New Zealand MP Keith Locke complained that his country's Waihopai spy base in Marlborough was being used as part of the US 'dirty tricks campaign'.[10] He pointed to Echelon's worldwide programme to intercept electronic communications shared by listeners in the United States, United Kingdom, Canada, Australia, and New Zealand.

'New Zealand could easily be helping the NSA intercept communications between UN delegates and their home countries,' Locke worried. Were US interests driving work at the Waihopai spy base? If so, what did that say about his country's foreign policy independence?

Echelon targets the United Nations. It collects e-mail and telephone information going to and from UN missions. Its largest installation is at Menwith Hill in Yorkshire. It seems incredible that Locke would be surprised by the possibility that Waihopai was involved with the business going on at Menwith and elsewhere in the network. What is credible is that Locke was surprised by the nature of this particular bit of it.

Shortly after the spy operation was revealed, France's foreign minister Dominique de Villepin, who had been lobbying anti-war support, left Paris to visit Cameroon, Angola, and Guinea, perhaps to commiserate with the three spy targets. Unknown to de Villepin was that UK Attorney General Lord Goldsmith had been receiving information about secret French negotiations.[11] France also was a target.

Among those deeply concerned about pressure applied in support of the war during this time were the archbishop of Canterbury, Rowan Williams, and Pope John Paul. The pope, actively fighting against a rush to war, would be revealed later as another target of US/UK spying. As for the archbishop, he said of Blair that the prime minister would account for himself 'at the "judgement seat"'.

'For Christians,' he added, 'that is the point of entry to heaven or to hell.'[12]

Tough talk for a man of the cloth.

The world press, except, of course, in the United States, had a field day reporting reactions to the 'dirty tricks' story and speculating about its impact on gaining broad-based support for a war so few seemed to want.

Five days after news of the NSA operation was published, in the midst of the ensuing storm, Attorney General Lord Goldsmith delivered to Tony Blair his formal opinion questioning the legality of a pre-emptive strike against Iraq without an authorizing resolution. It was an opinion researched and supported by his government's most senior legal advisers, including Elizabeth Wilmshurst.[13] Blair went back to Goldsmith; the opinion was not to his liking. On 17 March, quite a different opinion was delivered to Parliament and Blair happily told the world that launching a war against Iraq was unquestionably in accord with international law. Cautions raised in the original opinion had disappeared.

Loss of a UN Security Council resolution authorizing war led to three highly publicized resignations – those of Wilmshurst, Robin Cook as leader of the House of Commons, and Clare Short as Secretary of State for international development. The authors met with both Wilmshurst and Short in London; Cook declined to be interviewed.

Wilmshurst's resignation was straightforward and uncomplicated. She needed to leave her position because her views on the legitimacy of the Iraq action 'would not make it possible for me to continue my role as a Deputy Legal Adviser or my work more generally'. Leaving her senior government post after three decades was far from easy. Retired or not, the UK government continues to value her advice.[14] Now at Chatham House Royal Institute of International Affairs, she has no regrets about her resignation. There simply was no choice in the matter. Wilmshurst, impressive, painfully honest, is a woman of ethics, of high moral standards that are not subject to compromise.

Because one paragraph in Wilmshurst's letter of resignation was censored by the government 'in the public interest', there was enormous interest in just what that paragraph said. The full document was released by the BBC on 3 March 2005, under the Freedom of Information Act. The missing paragraph revealed that the attorney general's second opinion differed markedly from the first. With Wilmshurst, he had shared the belief that pre-emptive invasion of Iraq could be seriously open to legal challenge, even, although remotely, to war crimes charges. But his second, hurry-up opinion had switched to 'what is now the official line'. Details of what the original opinion contained would come later, when the prime minister was forced to reveal its full content.

On 17 March, the same day Blair announced that war would not be in violation of international law, Robin Cook delivered his resignation speech to the House of Commons. Applause for the resigning leader of the House was said to have been unprecedented. Cook was generous in his comments about the prime minister, expressing his hope that Blair would remain in office and making it clear he would not support those who wanted to use the current crisis to displace him. But Cook was clear in his opposition to Blair's determination to go to war. Cook, like Short, wanted UN approval and more time for alternatives, especially continued inspections.

'It is not France alone that wants more time for inspections,' Cook said. Germany wanted more time, as did Russia. There was not the necessary international support for abandoning alternatives to war. 'The reality is that Britain is being asked to embark on a war without agreement in any of the international bodies of which we are a leading partner – not NATO, not the European Union, and now, not the Security Council.

'Only a year ago,' Cook said, 'we and the United States were part of a coalition against terrorism that was wider and more diverse than I would ever have imagined possible.' Sadly, he noted, 'History will be astonished at the diplomatic miscalculations that led so quickly to the disintegration of that powerful coalition.'

Cook said he would resign if the United States and the United Kingdom went ahead with their planned pre-emptive attack, and he did promptly, as promised. A year later, looking back with no regrets, he said, 'President Bush was definite and apocalyptic,' quoting the president as having claimed that 'Saddam is building and hiding weapons that could enable him to intimidate the civilized world.'[15]

It was different with Clare Short, and she suffered for that difference. Short, head of the Department for International Development (DfID), had declared her intention to resign from Blair's cabinet if the attack took place without UN approval, but she did not, at least not immediately. Convinced that her efforts were needed in getting a UN mandate for reconstruction and the subsequent redevelopment of Iraq, she decided to stay on – even to the degree of supporting Blair's decision to invade. War was now inevitable, and attention should be turned toward post-war exigencies. Without the necessary mandate and broad international support, the victors would simply be occupiers, rather than implementers of a new political system, protectors of the citizenry, builders of a new infrastructure.

In spite of focusing on reconstruction, Short was active in last-minute attempts to avoid war, meeting with Blair, pleading for more time. One of those attempts involved an anti-war plan conceived in the United States by a federation of churches. A federation leader, evangelical minister Jim Wallis, had called Short in February asking to bring a delegation united against the war to London. She was immediately supportive.

The church delegation had an alternative, a five-point plan worth serious attention. It had purchased advertisements in newspapers, but the American public was not responding, its attention captured by a constant White House spin. How bizarre that the policies of George Bush and company, who had taken ownership of 'values' and Christian faith, were so challenged by dedicated believers in both.

The church plan included a process for deposing Saddam by indictment for war crimes and crimes against humanity, intensifying WMD inspections, fostering a democratic Iraq, organizing immediate and massive humanitarian efforts for Iraq, and implementing the road map to a Palestinian state by 2005.

It sounded good to Short, better than what was coming from Downing Street or Pennsylvania Avenue, but it appeared that neither occupant of those addresses was interested. They were packed for the trip to Baghdad.

Because she did not resign when the attack against Iraq was launched, Short was widely criticized for flip-floppy behaviour. On 12 May, after the war was a 'mission accomplished', she did leave the cabinet. As was true with both Wilmshurst and Cook, there seemed to be no other choice. She had no UN mandate for reconstruction in hand, which, given her DfID responsibilities, was of critical import. Further, she had no doubt that Blair had lied to her on numerous occasions.

She writes, 'I was absolutely clear I had to leave the government. Blair had failed to restrain the US rush to war and then broken his promise on internationalising reconstruction. The situation in the Middle East was disastrous and the behaviour of the Prime Minister indefensible.'[16]

Blair accepted Short's resignation, offering compliments for her work as head of DfID, but also questioning her complaint about 'internationalising' reconstruction of a defeated Iraq. He said he was working on getting a UN mandate. Why was she questioning him?

Short has spoken candidly about the run-up to the war and the American involvement, more so than any other member of her government. Although she left the cabinet, her constituents continue to elect her to office. She is loved, despised, praised, and castigated, depending upon the eye of the beholder. It is not difficult to determine the view in Blair's eye. Asked about her ensuing relationship with the prime minister, she told the authors, 'There isn't any.' When they happen to run into each other in one hallway or another, he 'simply looks away'.

What is most amazing is that within the United States, Britain's partner in war and peace, almost no notice was taken of the enormous upheaval across the Atlantic, an upheaval placed at Washington's doorstep by much of the world community. Clearly visible, parked at that same doorstep, was the outrageous violation of international law and ethics perpetrated by the United States in its spy operation designed to coerce support for an unpopular war.

How could America fail to notice what was happening abroad? How could it fail to care? Perhaps, just perhaps, because that failure was carefully and skilfully engineered.

CHAPTER 7: Silence in Washington

At some moments in history, when war and peace hang in the balance, journalism delayed is journalism denied.
                                          – Norman Solomon, 10 March 2003

O N THE SUNDAY the *Observer* broke the story of Frank Koza's message to GCHQ, 2 March 2003, Martin Bright received telephone calls from several major US news sources, including NBC, Fox News, and CNN. The callers were so excited, so eager to do their own reports, that they ordered cars to collect Martin from his home or wherever he might be at any given moment and rush him to interviews at various London locations. In short order, each called back and apologetically cancelled. Sorry, Mr Bright, we won't be covering the story. To this day, Martin cannot believe what happened.

'We're still scratching our heads. It was amazing.'

It was inevitable, given instantaneous communication across the Atlantic, that the White House would be asked about the Koza story. Unfortunately, spokesman Ari Fleischer explained, nobody in Washington could respond to questions concerning national security matters – not anyone from the administration, defence, or any of the intelligence agencies (of course), or anyone involved in international law issues. Lips were zipped shut. But even the silence was not a subject for media attention. Few were concerned about Washington's failure to respond to questions, or even about questions that might have been raised.

Three days after Bright and company's revelations appeared in the *Observer*, *The Times* called the Koza fiasco 'an embarrassing disclosure' and 'the most recent setback' in the US effort to gain support for war against Iraq. Newspapers elsewhere in the world carried the shameful story, including the outrage expressed by various UN delegations. By this time, the story had legs and was big news. Except within the United States, which was responsible for its existence.

The profound silence in Washington and across the United States was deafening. The absolute quiet smothered what would have been breaking news of an egregious error in judgement and of a tragic failure of the national ethic. In the always chaotic, cacophonous media centres of the US, a story exploding in headlines around the world was ignored. Such an embarrassment was this particular spying operation, with its attendant apparent international blackmail implications, that the whole business was immediately deep-sixed or, perhaps, studied and discussed and then deep-sixed.

But this is not supposed to happen in the United States! A free, independent media serves as a watchdog in cases like this. The various media make their own decisions about what to report and what not to report, and keeping the government honest is assumed to be a cornerstone of journalistic endeavour. Unless, of course, the issue involved is national security, which, it seems, has come to include everything the administration does not want to see in print or watch on the evening news. In these cases, the assumption fails.

Blacked out, then, are distracting images like flag-draped coffins returning from Iraq, or the most seriously wounded of thousands still in military hospitals. Exceptions to the latter are poignant photo ops of half a dozen carefully chosen injured who are guaranteed to greet their commander in chief with thankful, brave smiles. Now and again something goes terribly wrong, however, like photos of sexually abused Iraqi prisoners of war that reach the general public. There is no question that 'national security' has become the reason-of-choice to protect the citizenry from questionable government behaviour.

During World War II, for the most part, the news media cooperated fully with the government in withholding war-related information considered vital. 'National security' had a more precise definition, one easily understood and widely accepted. It was all-out war, with issues more militarily than politically defined. A veteran broadcaster reflected on this earlier media–government relationship when asked by the authors about the lack of coverage of the Frank Koza story. His response was simple.

'I was surprised they still have that power.'

The 'nation's newspaper', the prestigious *New York Times*, failed to tell its readers that a message had been sent from the National Security Agency asking British colleagues at GCHQ to take part in what the rest of the world was calling 'dirty tricks in high places'. Very high, given the frantic push at Downing Street and the White House to secure a UNSC resolution to legitimize a pre-emptive strike on Iraq.

At the time, writer and political pundit Norman Solomon asked the *New York Times* about covering the story.

'Well, it's not that we haven't been interested,' Alison Smale, the newspaper's deputy foreign editor, told him. The decision had been made not to 'relay' the *Observer* story. 'We would normally expect to do our own intelligence reporting.'

Oh? And where was this reporting? 'We are still definitely looking into it. It's not that we're not,' Smale explained. Apparently in the process of 'looking into it', the *New York Times* could get neither 'comment nor confirmation' from US officials, hardly surprisingly, and hardly a reason not to do said intelligence reporting of its own.

One would think that the *Washington Post* would have leaped on the story, for it is from Washington that news about the US government emanates. But there was no leap, only a short tiptoe on 4 March, day three of the leaked news. On page A17, sufficiently far back from Really Important Happenings, the *Post* carried in its final edition a 480-word account head-lined 'Spying Report No Shock to the UN', a ho-hum piece noting that spying on the United Nations was an old sport with lots of players. This new adventure was hardly worth serious attention.

Ironically, on the very day of the *Observer* story, the *Post*'s Anne-Marie Slaughter wrote a commentary for the Washington paper headlined 'Accused of Irrelevance and Deeply Divided Over Iraq, the United Nations Has Never Mattered More'.

Observed Slaughter, 'Whatever their stance on a war in Iraq, policy makers and pundits seem to agree on one thing: The present crisis puts the relevance and credibility of the United Nations on the line.' It would seem that the *Post*, noting the 'relevance and credibility' of the United Nations, might find the Koza story worthy of greater attention than it received.

The *Post* continued to report on the heated UN debate over war against Iraq as the week went on. Strong opposition by France, Germany, and Russia was noted, but no mention was made of the outrage expressed about the NSA operation. Five days after the *Observer* story, the *Post* carried the word that 'Bush Is Ready to Go Without UN; But US to Seek Security Council Vote Next Week'. Again, there was nothing said about the fact that Angola, Cameroon, Chile, Bulgaria, Guinea, and Pakistan, the specific NSA targets, were fiercely angry at the United States and that chances of getting favourable votes from these swing nations were now nil.

At the end of the week Senator Joseph Biden Jr, the ranking Democrat on the Senate Foreign Relations Committee, wrote an op-ed piece for the *Post*, urging passage of the proposed, hotly debated UN resolution. 'France, Russia and Germany are engaged in a game of dangerous brinkmanship at the United Nations,' he warned. 'Some in the Bush administration have responded in kind.' (If he considered the spy operation an exercise in brinkmanship, Biden refrained from specifics, and his office has failed to respond to the authors about his thinking at the time.) 'Together, they threaten to drive the interests of our countries over a cliff.'

The senator held out hope that there was 'still time to pull back from the precipice and disarm Iraq without dividing the Atlantic alliance and debilitating the Security Council'. But the Security Council had already been debilitated, and the interests of the country, in the form of the desired resolution, had already disappeared over the cliff.

What little attention was paid by the US media to the published leak focused entirely on the theme of the *Post* story. Everyone knows everyone has spied on the United Nations. Daily sweeping of offices takes place to ensure that bugs are exterminated. Conversations of substance are held in sealed rooms or in public parks. So, what was new about the Koza story? On 4 March, the *Los Angeles Times* carried a piece on the story, with the same theme. Bottom line: so what?

'Forgery or no [the Koza e-mail], some say it's nothing to get worked up about,' assured the Los Angeles paper. The 'purported' spy memo could add to US troubles at the United Nations, the article conceded; however, as is so well known, this sort of spying has gone on since the United Nations was founded in 1945. It's just more of the same old stuff – so what's new?

What was new, once again, was the intent behind the spying, an intent that had all of the characteristics of big money black-mail, of setting up a scheme whereby two powerful nations could claim the backing of a strong, willing coalition, when coercion rather than cooperation had been the key.

There is also the matter of intimidation. Bright's co-author Ed Vulliamy noted that although people around the world were furious over the US plot to manipulate Security Council votes, 'Almost all governments are extremely reluctant to speak up against the [NSA-initiated] espionage. This further illustrates their vulnerability to the US government.'

If that vulnerability kept 'official' complaints from being filed by governments, individuals from foreign nations were speaking up in unofficial fury and anger. Here were news stories that merited huge headlines. Foreign diplomats were raging about the US violation of international law. The country's reputation as leader of the free world, as a government of integrity and moral correctness was sorely sullied. There was plenty to write about. The problem was that Washington did not want to hear this discouraging news and certainly did not want the American public to be bothered with it as well.

The implication here is that official Washington was un-officially able to influence major media sources with regard to publicizing the Koza caper. What other reason would there be for the abrupt change of plans to interview Martin Bright immediately following publication of his story? For simply ignoring an international brouhaha of enormous proportion that so directly affected the US and its interests? Yet one must admit that this inference could be entirely wrong. No such evidence to support it was found. It could have been a matter of extraordinary coincidence that both the Bush administration and the nation's most prestigious media agreed that the spy operation, and the ensuing international outrage, did not merit public attention.

CHAPTER 8: Taiwan Calling

A 28-year-old woman employee at GCHQ was arrested last week by Gloucestershire police and released on bail. A GCHQ spokesman declined to give further details . . . The leak of the memo reflects deep unease throughout Whitehall about the Bush administration's conduct in the growing Iraq crisis. It is severely embarrassing to GCHQ and to Tony Blair at a time of widespread doubts about the morality of an invasion of Iraq.
– Jeevan Vasagar and Richard Norton-Taylor,
Guardian, 10 March 2003

T HE WOMAN ARRESTED was not publicly named. Her identity was kept secret for months – at first, even from her family.

'I was released from police custody on Thursday at lunch-time. I went home and immediately called my parents in Taiwan and told them that I was in a bit of trouble, but I didn't tell them that I had leaked the memo or that I had been arrested. It was only when they read the *Guardian* story about the arrest of a 28-year-old woman at GCHQ the next week that they put it all together. I didn't tell my grandmother or any of my relatives until at least the day my parents realized the truth and called me.'

In Taiwan, Katharine Gun's father, Paul Harwood, read the

10 March *Guardian* on the Internet, intensely interested in the follow-up story about the leak of Frank Koza's message, which had appeared the Sunday before. Now the story was linked to GCHQ, where his daughter worked.

On the Sunday before, Harwood had seen the original *Observer* story, 'Revealed: US Dirty Tricks to Win Vote on Iraq War', and called it to the attention of his wife and son, shocked that the United States would make such an egregious, politically damaging misstep in its campaign for war.

UK citizens, the Harwoods worried that British intelligence had joined in the spy operation, and now they wondered if the person who leaked the document was someone Katharine might know. Jan Harwood says her husband and son followed the news of the 'dirty tricks leak like hawks'.[1]

Paul expected to hear explosive media reaction to the GCHQ leak coming from other news sources – particularly those from the United States. He followed the story on BBC shortwave radio and the Internet, but the expected US pickup did not happen. He watched CNN. The 'news void', as he calls it, left him amazed and angry.

'The only reference to the story that I can recall in the following days was a programme – I think it was called *International Correspondent* – on CNN. The presenter said there were rumours of US spying on the United Nations. It was just a very brief reference when he was talking to an ambassador from an African country.'

Paul recalls that the interview was taking place in a conference room at UN headquarters. 'The ambassador was asked, "Do you know anything about this?" And he made a joke of it, he laughed! He had a tape recorder on the desk, and said, "The United States is listening to me do this?" More laughter, and that was it. The whole thing took about forty seconds. I thought, What the hell's going on here? This is a major story and why isn't it all over, everywhere?'

Paul wanted the world to know about the NSA spy operation. This, of course, was before he learned of Katharine's part in it. Later, he found the prospect of publicity surrounding Katharine 'alarming'.

It was five days after the first story broke that Katharine telephoned and spoke to her mother. 'She told Jan that she'd been suspended from work for something she had done,' Paul says. 'She didn't say what it was, but said she thought we would approve. Then, when I saw the story about a 28-year-old woman's arrest, it wasn't a big leap, putting two and two together. I nearly went through the roof. I thought, my God, it's her!'

Katharine's mother came home from church that Sunday to find her husband at the computer, this latest article on the screen. 'It's our Katharine!' he told her. Jan Harwood says she was 'thunderstruck', and that she and Paul were 'kind of kicking ourselves for not realizing immediately that Katharine was in deep trouble'. But the earlier call had not implied anything very serious, perhaps some minor infraction of employment rules.

Once the dots were connected that day, the Harwoods wanted desperately to talk with their daughter. There were so many questions to be asked, and, of course, assurances to be given. Because of the time difference between Taiwan and Cheltenham, they suffered through an agonizing wait before placing the call.

It was enormously helpful that Katharine did not have to say, 'I did it,' to her parents when they called. It was they who said the words.

'We know it was you.'

In the minutes to follow, Jan and Paul Harwood promised wholehearted support. They let Katharine know of their pride in her and in what she had done. They understood, they told her. Fully, completely. Clearly, the Harwoods' daughter had figured her parents' reaction correctly when, in the earlier telephone conversation with her mother, she said she thought they would approve of the 'something' she had done that had got her into 'a bit of trouble'.

'We did, absolutely,' her father says. 'We gave her full backing from the start. We knew that whatever she did she did for good reason.' Her mother's reaction was an enthusiastic 'Good for her!'

A blatant breach of international law for such a sordid purpose by the United States (and likely, they surmised, by Great Britain as well) was unacceptable; yet their daughter's lawbreaking in protest was not only acceptable to both parents, it was also courageous, astonishingly heroic. Much later, shortly before Katharine's 2004 appearance at the Old Bailey, her mother would speak publicly about Katharine's leaking the infamous e-mail. 'I am deeply proud of what my daughter did to reveal wrongdoing on the part of the US and British governments.'

For now, the world was still in the dark about the identity of the twenty-eight-year-old intelligence officer arrested in Cheltenham.

Jan Harwood admitted thinking that the situation 'could be a bit tricky' for her daughter but was still proud and completely supportive. She would not allow herself to become consumed with worry, as many mothers might have done. No point in being frantic about what might happen.

'Sufficient unto the day is the evil thereof,' Jan says. 'A lot of it comes down to basic personality. I'm not a natural worrier; I only face a problem as and when it needs to be faced. I won't waste psychic energy in thinking about what might happen.' Her husband is 'a bigger worrier'. She adds, 'He was more scared than I was.'

Less than two weeks after the *Guardian* story reporting the arrest of a twenty-eight-year-old GCHQ employee, a US-led token coalition launched a pre-emptive strike on Iraq. Katharine Gun would be the new war's first British casualty.

Legal representation was a major concern for both Katharine and her parents and the subject of frequent communication between England and Taiwan. It was clear that the duty solicitor assigned to Katharine's case would have to be replaced by someone more experienced in this aspect of criminal law.

During this first week after her release, Katharine learned

that the *Guardian* news group, to which the *Observer* belonged, felt obliged to pay for her defence. A tempting offer, given her limited financial circumstances, but she declined. 'I didn't want to be beholden to a newspaper.'

Katharine's other option was her employee union. As a paid-up member of the Public and Civil Services Union, she was entitled to representation by the union's legal staff. But the union solicitors were employment, not criminal, specialists, hardly appropriate for her case.

It was at this point that Katharine learned of Liberty's interest in her.[2] The non-profit human rights organization made contact through Katharine's union, and a meeting with Liberty director John Wadham followed. Union legal staff would assist with employment issues, but Liberty would become her criminal case solicitors. It was with profound relief that Katharine accepted Liberty's offer to defend her. 'If it hadn't been for Liberty we would have been sunk – swallowed up, chewed over, and spat out,' Paul Harwood says. 'And probably destitute to boot. Liberty was our salvation.'

It was time to tell others in her family about her arrest.

'And then I did tell my grandmother and my aunt, and my grandma said she would be happy to come down and stay with me, just to help keep my mind off things and to give me some company. So we agreed, and the following week she came down and spent some time with me, just puttering around the house, mostly. When Yasar had a free day, he would drive us into the country. Otherwise, we would walk into town along a pleasant tree-lined avenue with nice houses on either side.'

Katharine's silver-haired grandmother, her father's mum, is short, delightfully sprightly, warm, and intelligent. She is a caring, thoughtful person, just what her frightened granddaughter needed at the moment. The authors met her in Brighton, where she and her two charming sisters, Katharine's beloved great-aunts, were heading out for a festive lunch. Firm in their devotion to Katharine, one gets the feeling they would have taken on Inspector Tintin and the entire Crown Prosecution

Service, given half a chance. It was typical of Katharine's grand-mother that she searched for comforting moments in the garden at Cheltenham.

'As we foraged around, we uncovered a lovely path that had completely overgrown, and I remember we also bought some plants which my grandma helped me put in. Now we had a bit of colour in my garden!

'My grandma stayed for several days, a week or longer, and it was just so nice to have her around, to have her company. Of course, she was worried about what was going to happen to me. I was, too. At this stage none of us really knew what to expect. The limbo period had started and none of us would know how long it would last.'

PART III

THE WOMAN

CHAPTER 9: Eight Months in Limbo

Gun's existence was reduced to staying at home with the curtains drawn, plus occasional trips to the local coffee shop.
— *Evening Standard* (London), 27 May 2005, reflecting on 2003

I T WAS THE limbo period. But the *Evening Standard*'s picture of Katharine in hiding over the next weeks and months was exaggerated.

Yet this was an unquestionably frightening period for her and, at times, one of near-isolation. It was especially so at the beginning, when hours were made bearable only by the presence of family and two or three close friends. Later she would function well when she was alone, but for now people around her provided distraction and kept her imagination from constantly dwelling on the terrifying possibilities that loomed ahead.

During these early days and weeks, Katharine clung to the hope that she would not be charged and would not face prison. Perhaps, she thought, the government would not want to pursue the case, and she could 'just slip under the rug' of anonymity and emerge later in a different place, in a different role. No one need ever know. This was her imagination at its ultimate best, a scenario played out from time to time in an ephemeral mist of hope.

Yasar was quietly supportive, always there, always with her, his presence warm and comforting. It was difficult each day to see him climb into the Metro and drive off to work, leaving her behind. It was a moment of sad remembrance for Katharine, forced to relive those other mornings when they would leave the house together, and he would drop her off at GCHQ, mornings when she would have her cinnamon bun and coffee before settling down to the business of Mandarin translation.

Katharine still walked to meet her husband now and again after his workday was finished, but now she did so in a way to avoid running into former GCHQ colleagues. The couple seldom went out, except for rare occasions with a very few close friends. If anything, their marriage strengthened under the pressure of the unknown and treacherous landscape that lay before them.

Inspector Tintin came to call one stormy day, bringing along a colleague. The entrance to the Guns' home was at the side, a tiny space with a steep staircase leading immediately up to the bedrooms. Katharine, in her nightclothes, ran downstairs to open the door and found the two officers standing in the pouring rain.

'Hello, may we step inside?' the inspector asked.

Heart pounding, Katharine held open the door and the two officers crowded inside. Noting Katharine's nightwear, ever-kindly Tintin suggested she might want to go upstairs and get dressed; they would wait in the entryway until she was ready. Katharine thanked him, turned, and was partway up the stairs when the other officer, clearly looking up her gown, whistled softly. Furious, Tintin ordered him outside, where he remained, storm or no, throughout his supervisor's visit with Katharine.

The inspector's questions were few, a matter of routine checking. He collected a second mobile telephone; the first was taken during the initial search of the flat. Although he was non-threatening in manner, the fact that he was present, that New Scotland Yard would keep her on its screen, was threatening in itself. It brought home the vivid reality that had faded, if only slightly, in the garden with Katharine's grandmother.

Katharine learned to lie about her work status. Because GCHQ staff sometimes studied little-known languages at various 'off-campus' locations, perhaps for months at a time, learning in family homes or elsewhere, a missing linguist did not necessarily reflect disciplinary action. Still, she stayed away from GCHQ and places where she might find herself in the position of having to repeat what was a painfully uncomfortable lie.

'I continued to talk with my parents on the phone and it occurred to my mum, who wasn't teaching full time, that she could come to the UK much earlier than usual to spend time with me. Not long after my grandma left for home, in mid-April, Mum arrived – a good time for her, because she really loves Britain in the springtime, when the daffodils and all the flowers are out. It was a really superb spring that year. In fact, I remember that on the day my mum arrived, it was so warm that she hurried upstairs and dug a bathing suit out of her neatly packed suitcase so we could sit outside in the garden and enjoy the amazing summerlike springtime. And we did that for several days because it was such wonderful weather, and my mum is the queen of relaxation. She's quite happy just sitting and reading a book and doing very little. She thoroughly enjoyed that time I think, and also kept me – and my mind – occupied.'

Jan Harwood's calming presence in Cheltenham at this time was immeasurably valuable to Katharine, not only as a mother but also as a close friend, a companion with whom everything could be shared. Unflappable Jan was able to smooth some of the roughness of the pervasive not-knowing that was so depressing for Katharine.

Jan's motto, 'Sufficient unto the day is the evil thereof,' was serving her well. Her refusal to deal with a potential evil clouding their days and haunting their nights gave her the strength and forbearance to keep Katharine from succumbing to despair. 'There was absolutely no point in worrying about problems or disaster.' Whatever lay ahead for Katharine would be faced together. If Jan Harwood had any serious worries that spring, they were focused on her husband and his fear for Katharine. Jan would not anticipate the evil that might be ahead for all of them, but Paul would – and did.

While criminal court issues in the Gun case would fall under the aegis of the Crown Prosecution Service, employment issues would be adjudicated by the government's human resources administration at GCHQ. That the issues so categorized, employment and criminal, were essentially identical made the whole business infinitely more difficult for the offender. A single act would be judged in two different spheres.

On 5 March, the day of Katharine's arrest, she was suspended from duty 'pending the outcome of the police investigation'. She was kept on the payroll. In its formal but courteous notice of Precautionary Suspension from Duty, dated 6 March, a personnel officer writes, 'I am sure that you will appreciate that it would not be appropriate for you to attend work at this time.'

On 9 May, Katharine was formally notified by GCHQ of disciplinary charges against her and invited to respond. On the twenty-second of the month, John Wadham wrote to the agency's Mr Stephen Gale, who was assigned Katharine's case. Wadham's letter was cautious, acknowledging GCHQ's requirement that any response to the formal notification must come directly from Katharine 'without assistance from a legal advisor'. The solicitor emphasized that his correspondence was not intended to serve as her response, but rather to raise questions about certain concerns. Those concerns dealt directly with the entangled nature of the specific employment and criminal issues involved with Katharine's violation of the Official Secrets Act.

'Our central concern,' Wadham wrote, 'is that any submissions or statements that Katharine makes in these [employment] disciplinary proceedings are likely to be based on exactly the same material as her defence in any criminal proceedings.' In order to defend her job, Katharine might have to disclose material that could prejudice her criminal trial. Care must be taken, advised Wadham, to prevent this sort of prejudice. His lengthy and detailed letter, with specific citations and references to case law, concludes by asking for a suspension of disciplinary procedures 'subject to the determination of any criminal proceedings'.

Should Katharine not be charged, should there be no criminal case, such a delay could prove to be extremely helpful – in the unlikely possibility that anything could.

Fortunately for Katharine, her mother was still with her during these early days of dealing with the GCHQ administration. While there was no real hope of reinstatement or clearing of her record, Katharine knew the process of filing statements and making an appeal was necessary.

'I knew they wouldn't reinstate me, but it was a matter of following procedure. Liberty advised me to follow the routine that was open to me. They did, however, try to prevent GCHQ from dismissing me because they argued that it would prejudice a trial.'

Less than a week after Wadham wrote to GCHQ, the agency met with government lawyers in charge of the criminal case; the following day, Liberty was notified that Wadham's request for delay had been denied and the agency would proceed with the internal disciplinary hearing. It was 29 May.

That same evening, Katharine heard BBC broadcast journalist Andrew Gilligan quote a 'senior government source' who claimed that Number 10 Downing Street 'probably knew' the now-suspect 45-minute claim was wrong. The broadcast would launch an intense political storm, with fervent denials, over manipulation of intelligence to support the Iraq War. Tonight, one listener painfully familiar with the concept of intelligence manipulation was especially interested in Gilligan's report. She was about to be ejected, formally, eternally, from the intelligence community.

On 11 June, the GCHQ disciplinary board convened, with Katharine present. On the advice of counsel, Katharine refused to answer the board's questions. Her position, as presented to those who would judge her, was that participation in the hearing could jeopardize her criminal trial. Made clear from the beginning was a line carefully drawn on the basis of the distinction between employment and criminal issues.

Thus, agency disciplinary action against employee Katharine Gun was not that she had breached the Official Secrets Act, but rather that she had acted 'in contravention of service as a GCHQ employee'. The distinction was hardly helpful. In any event, what was happening now was only phase one, loss of her job. In a sense, it was a rehearsal for what would be in store for her down the line, perhaps loss of her freedom.

Katharine was notified of the board's decision on 13 June. It was exactly what she expected; she was officially out of work, officially off the payroll. She would appeal, for the purpose of exhausting the last option open to her, knowing that her appeal would be denied. She was complying with Liberty's advice to take this final step with her former employer.

It was clear that money problems for the Gun household were about to increase significantly. Even with Liberty defending her pro bono, there were growing personal expenses associated with her case, including trips to London. Yasar's café job paid a living wage, but nothing more. Katharine needed work, but seeking any kind of regular employment at the moment was unrealistic. Potential employers would ask questions she could not answer.

A possible solution to the money problem arrived in Katharine's letterbox while her mother was still visiting. The two decided that what was offered might just do the trick, given that it was a business opportunity – essentially an independent operation without troublesome personnel applications and job interviews.

'I got a little printed card, obviously from someone who was leafleting the area, and it was about a job opportunity. It was a source of income for people who were fed up with a nine-to-five work style, or who had been made redundant,' Katharine says. 'It turned out that it was for a network marketing opportunity for a company that is very well established in the United States, and also growing around the world. It's a company that bases all of its products on aloe vera.'

With her mother, Katharine explored, and even launched, the direct-marketing venture that would soon fail. The business model is a good one, she believes, but came to realize that it works only for someone with the ability to develop a good marketing base, someone with abundant friends and the personal contacts this sort of enterprise demands. At the time, she had neither. Although her professional experience with the direct-sales company was short-lived, Katharine and her husband remain close to the woman who put the little card in her letterbox and started her in business.

'She's been very supportive of us and of my case,' Katharine says.

The business opportunity failed, but it brought Katharine the satisfaction of doing something. It gave her a 'feeling of purpose, and it was good to be involved with something. I remember going up to the talks at the headquarters, based in a really lovely manor house in its own grounds. Everybody was pleasant, so helpful.'

What Katharine missed most about the failed enterprise was not the time spent at the manor house, or the peaceful drive there, but the mental space occupied by the business. It was now vacant, like an empty store with its front windows papered over. It was necessary to fill that space or the image would change, the papered windows replaced by bars.

Katharine was trying to earn money and to find a niche, even a temporary one, where she could experience a sense of belonging. She missed GCHQ, something far more than merely a place of work. It was a way of life that came with built-in friendships and shared lifestyles. Although it was a jealous master, dictating how one should think and feel and demanding one's blind obedience, it was also comforting in many ways, a protective parent. One belonged to GCHQ; one was not just employed by it.

Loneliness was like a recurring illness. There were times when Katharine was able to stand being alone, could deal with the emptiness in her life. She tried to think of things to keep her busy, to avoid the sickening fear and worry. Her mother returned to the family home in Durham to prepare for summer guests, and Katharine missed her sorely. Whenever possible, she made the train trip to Durham, where she was surrounded by family.

Troubling news about the misuse of intelligence to support military action against Iraq continued to surface, news Katharine followed closely. Tony Blair was emphatic: Intelligence had not been manipulated for political purposes. In the United States, two Senate committees launched inquiries into possible abuse of intelligence. Frank Koza was only one player revealed in this high-stakes game of intelligence manipulation. There would be many to follow.

As an observer of the unfolding scene, and with the possibility of her own public exposure, Katharine was in a place of reflection. What had she done and at what cost to herself and her family? If she could go back to the morning she printed out Koza's message, would she behave differently, perhaps delete the NSA invitation to conspiracy? Absolutely not. Her answer was the same then as it is now.

'I would do it again. I would do it all over again!'

An appeal of the disciplinary board's decision was filed on Katharine's behalf on 26 June. On 11 July, the appeal was heard and on 18 July, it was denied. The board's decision to deny was affirmed in a detailed letter from GCHQ's new director, David Pepper. Meticulously, the Pepper letter reviews each of three grounds for appeal. The bottom line: Katharine's failure to participate in the original hearing was insufficient reason to bypass this required step in the dismissal process; there were no irregularities in the way the board carried out its role; and, last, it was not wrong for GCHQ to dismiss Katharine in light of her statement of guilt.

It was finally over. Relief was mixed with sadness.

'But then, things changed. I went down to a café where I used to go every day, on my way into town. There were a couple of postgrad students who lived above the coffee shop and used the shop almost as their own living room. I would bump into them now and again. I didn't tell them the truth about me. At this time, I still wasn't telling anybody outside my immediate family and intimate circle of friends about what had happened. I was so hoping that they wouldn't charge me and that nobody would ever know! I was telling the white lie, saying I was studying another language, that what I was doing was classified, and I couldn't tell them any more than that. As far as I could tell, my story seemed to go down very easily with most people, although, after a while, I think it started to look a bit fishy. I don't know what people really thought at the time, whether they suspected that I was the person who had been suspended from GCHQ. No one ever said.

'But anyway, I had a chat with these postgrad students about the possibility of actually leaving GCHQ to go back to school. They gave me a prospectus, a magazine specifically for gradu-ates and postgraduates. In it I saw an advert for a course at the University of Birmingham, in the study of global ethics. It just really intrigued me. The concept of global ethics was refreshing, something I would find very interesting.

'I decided to apply for the course.

'My parents were very supportive. My husband, on the other hand, wasn't quite sure what it was about, and I found it hard to try to explain the concept of global ethics in English, not knowing how to say it in Turkish. I remember looking it up in our Turkish–English dictionary but still couldn't make it really clear. I'm not sure he really understood what I was on about! And I think he was also thinking from a more practical point of view and didn't really see how it would be all that useful. It was also pretty expensive, for British standards, and it would mean commuting to the department for my classes, also an expense. In the end, he agreed because it seemed like something I really wanted to do.

'I would start my work for a master's degree in global ethics in September!'

By now, Katharine's father had arrived from Taiwan for his annual United Kingdom visit, joining her mother at the family home in Durham. Together, they travelled down to Cheltenham to stay with Katharine and Yasar. She drove them around the summery green Cotswolds and took them to pubs in the countryside. There was, during these weeks, a sense of peace she had not known for some time. There were enjoyable things to do, and the days were filled. Katharine and her father had time together, a blessing for both. The visit was all too short.

'When I was sitting at home on my own, when nothing particular was happening, when I had no one to spend time with, no one to talk to, it was hard. But there were times when I seemed to be quite happy being on my own, and I coped well with the solitude. That may come from my being an only child until I was six.

'After the summer holiday, I began to travel up to Birmingham for two days a week for the start of my master's degree. I remember the first day we got together, when we had to introduce ourselves to each other. It was not a very large group – there were only about ten or eleven of us sitting around in a circle in this cool, breezy classroom introducing ourselves to each other. When it came to me, I was very nervous talking about myself.

'By this stage I didn't feel like I was the same person as before. The person I was had been submerged by this huge amount of pressure and uncertainty. So I felt "nervy" around people, even though I don't think I gave off that impression. Inside, however, I felt cautious and suspicious all the time.

'In my introduction, I told the other students that I used to work at GCHQ. I really can't remember if I told them that I'd been sacked or that I left voluntarily. I certainly didn't tell

them about the leak or that I was responsible for it. I just kind
of joked that later on in the year I might be arrested and put
in prison. I said it deliberately and in a joking manner, just to
kind of ease the tension, because I felt that what I was saying
was a bit confusing, a bit awkward. I'm not sure I made sense.

'As it happened, joking about being arrested and put in
prison kind of prepared the students for what did happen.
Suddenly the woman they knew sitting in their classrooms was
everywhere in the news. That's when they learned the truth.

'It had been so enjoyable, the first three-quarters of the term.
I liked the subject, and have always liked being in an environment that is both sociable and mentally stimulating. I liked the
people and am still in contact with some of them. Good people.
Maybe that's what drew them to the subject matter of the
global ethics course.'

Suddenly, with one day's warning, it was all over –
Birmingham, Katharine's tantalizing dream, her fervent hope
for the future.

The eight-month limbo period ended with a bang. A bombshell, according to the media.

CHAPTER 10: The Third-Culture Kid

When I was expecting Katharine, I was so hoping for a girl!
We have a strong mother-daughter tradition in my family, and
both my mother and grandmother died before Katharine was
born. I wanted a daughter!

The tradition, the relationship, was important to me.

– Jan Harwood, to the authors, June 2005

THE LITTLE GIRL, a preschooler, sat on the floor with
playmates, her surroundings warm and welcoming and
wonderfully Chinese in both decor and spirit – immaculate, pleasing to the eye, vaguely and exotically scented. The
child was happy, content, except for the obvious mistake God
had made in her life. Her hair was blonde, her skin far too pale
for her liking, and her eyes disturbingly round – that is, compared
to those of the children around her.

She was not Chinese, and she desperately wanted to be.
Not that she wished for different parents or would insist that
they, too, be Chinese. The problem was solely with her. Her
friends were Chinese, and she, bright-eyed and curious, by
now was speaking and understanding their native tongue. Their
lifestyle was as familiar as that in her own home, another lovely,

well-appointed house with an ornately tiled roof and charming, tree-lined inner courtyard.

Grown-up Katharine Gun, expert in Mandarin, clearly remembers wanting to be Chinese when she was a child. Although there were Western children in her life, she identified more with her native friends. She was, and still is, infinitely comfortable with the people and their culture. More comfortable, as it would turn out when she went to England for boarding school, than with those in the land of her birth.

To know the grown-up Katharine, the woman who now has a place in history, is to know the lifestyle of the child who wanted to be Chinese and the shy teenager who went halfway around the world to attend a strange and intimidating boarding school. It is necessary to know the Katharine who became a teacher in Japan and who, ultimately, entered the cloak-and-dagger world of the British secret service.

'Taiwan was an ideal place to bring up young children,' Paul Harwood says of the historic and exceptionally beautiful university campus where Katharine spent most of her childhood and where her parents still live. 'Had we been living off campus, in the holey-moley of a Taiwanese situation, we probably could not have endured it. Especially with small children. But I have to say we were not living in the real world – the real Taiwanese world – because there we were on this marvellous campus.

'At the time we arrived there, I suppose the Taiwan economic miracle had begun, but it was only in the initial stages. Life was simpler and safer. Very few people had cars at that time – perhaps two or three people on the campus, and it was quite a big campus. Children walking or riding bicycles could use the streets without worry. Other dangers one might imagine threatening young children running free in the neighbourhood simply did not exist. There were no concerns about kidnapping or strangers with abuse in mind.'

At a far younger age than most Western children, Katharine was allowed freedom to visit friends and explore the neighbourhood. 'When she was in first grade,' Jan Harwood remembers, 'Katharine could cycle to school safely. Sometimes we wouldn't see her for hours on end, but we knew she would be in a friend's home or in the gardens.'

Katharine and her younger brother, Mike, were a key factor in the Harwoods' decision to remain in Taiwan after an initial two-year commitment to teach at Tunghai University. Katharine was three years old when her father, teaching French in his native Britain, decided to pack up wife and toddler and pursue the dream that had been his for so long.

For Paul, it was a matter of education – his, not that of his students – that led the family to Taiwan. 'I think it was mostly that I felt my whole education and my entire teaching experience had been within the Western European sphere.'

This is not what the younger Paul had in mind when he was first thinking about university studies. 'When I was applying for university, I had thoughts of doing an Oriental language.' No one but Paul seemed to think this was an especially good idea, and, he says, 'I hadn't at the time the courage to insist and go for it.'

A keen interest in Oriental studies remained with Paul, always somewhere in the back of his mind and surfacing now and again as serious temptation. After six years of teaching in England – mainly French language and literature, along with some German courses – Paul had had enough of not doing what he really wanted to do. 'I thought, my God, I cannot go on doing this for another thirty years!' The answer was a change in direction, a return to university and an escape from the 'European sphere'.

Escape meant Paul was limited to Durham, home of a school of Oriental studies. To go elsewhere would have been financially impossible, and Durham was a respectable choice. 'Had there been a course in Sanskrit I might well have opted for that, but there was not. There was a course in Indian civilization but no language.' The Chinese course offered exactly what Paul wanted. Plus, 'even at that point I had a certain interest in the East from a spiritual point of view. And so that's what I did, and that led to us being in Taiwan.'

When the Harwoods moved to Taiwan in the seventies, it was still a very agrarian culture. Katharine remembers the main road from the hilltop campus as 'kind of a wide dirt track, and there were bamboo fields and sugar-cane crops and rice paddies all the way down to the city'. Even as a small child peering from the window of a bus wobbling its way into town, Katharine found the landscape both lovely and fascinating.

For Katharine's mother, teaching at the university proved to be interesting and satisfying. Especially so, because the administration was quite willing to schedule the teaching couple's classes so that one parent was home at all times. It was an ideal arrangement, one that 'couldn't be beaten', Jan says. 'I never needed daycare for the children, with Paul teaching in the afternoons and me teaching in the mornings.' Jan and Paul were involved in university activities, and their young daughter was involved and totally happy with her Chinese playmates. Social activities for the Harwood family included going out once a week for a special evening meal. There were some adjustments, but nothing serious except, perhaps, giving up coffee, an unaffordable luxury. 'The cost of a jar of instant coffee was ridiculous!' Jan complains.

For Paul, a significant advantage at this time was the ability to be both student and teacher. He began studies in the Chinese Literature Department, his plan to acquire the background and qualifications necessary to teach the subject in Great Britain at some point in the future.

'And so, I started my studies and did three semesters in the graduate programme. I got about half the credits towards a master's degree. But then, at that point, our son Mike was born. I was teaching at Tunghai and commuting to take a class in Taipei. But then in December of that first semester of the second year, Mike was born prematurely. Jan was taken into a neighbouring town, to a Christian hospital there.

'The birth was actually arrested by administering a drug, and so for a couple of weeks, which were absolutely crucial, his birth was delayed.' It was a difficult period, with Jan in the hospital, Paul dividing his time among the hospital, teaching, and studying, and Katharine in the care of friends and neighbours. In the end, Paul chose to focus on his family and teaching and put aside the master's degree programme.

If her parents were exhausted during this time, Katharine was not. She was active, busy with school, busy with her friends. Too, there was a charming little brother worthy of her attention. She felt very grown up at six. And quite independent.

Katharine began school life at the Tunghai University kindergarten, initially established for the children of the university's professors. She did well and then moved into a distinctly more difficult academic life – five years of tough primary school in the Chinese system. Each year in this highly competitive environment was increasingly difficult. What Jan and Paul eventually discovered was that Taiwanese parents put their children into special schools during the summer, where they study all of the material to be covered in class the coming semester. After five years, it was just too much of a struggle, too demanding, even for the daughter of a pair of teachers. To her credit, a determined Katharine kept up with her classmates and survived in the foreign system longer, her father believes, than any other Western child. Her brother lasted one year, fitting the norm for foreign students.

All of Katharine's classes had been taught in Chinese. With her transfer to Morrison Academy, a nearby Christian school originally intended for the children of American missionaries serving in Taiwan, she would be taught in English. Scholastic competition was not nearly so severe at Morrison, but there were certain drawbacks. Among them, the fact that, for the most part, Katharine's classmates were not Chinese. She was not the only child with blonde hair, light skin, and eyes that were not almond-shaped.

A more troubling drawback, at least for Katharine's parents, was the academy's ultra-conservative Christian environment. At Morrison, there was no school prom, as dancing was not allowed; instead there was a graduation banquet. The school's library was strictly limited to books that fitted its evangelical mission. Harry Potter, with his witches and magic, would never have made it over the threshold.

There were positive aspects about the Morrison experience. The academy was small, with a student enrolment of approximately four hundred, and offered a strong programme of extracurricular activities. Katharine was involved in both sports and drama, and she sang in the Morrison choir. She studied piano but not very seriously, although her parents bought a piano for her.

'Katharine got a pretty strong indoctrination in the Christian ethic at Morrison,' her father says. But the extreme nature of the school's theological philosophy led to the Harwoods finding it necessary to 'counter somewhat' its narrow teachings. They were not alone in this regard. Other parents, even some who were missionaries, were concerned about achieving a philosophical balance in their children's education.

There is no question that the family's spiritual experience was decidedly mixed. Katharine attended Sunday school 'when she was seven, eight, nine', according to her father, and 'there was a young people's Christian fellowship' to which she belonged as a teenager. 'The children would meet on Saturday evenings and go up the hill and eat ice cream.' Katharine, amused, recalls her relationship to the church and its activities as having been somewhat more substantial than ice cream on a hilltop.

'Taiwan is a twenty-four-hour society, and what my dad remembers about ice cream on the hillside were the midnight trips my church friends and I sometimes took up to the student village above the campus to eat slush ices with red bean paste and tapioca-type balls. It was great fun, all part of a lovely childhood.

'I remember being confirmed in Taiwan. I can't remember if I was baptized at the same time, or whether that was done as a child. But when I was about thirteen, I decided to be confirmed in the Episcopal Church where my mum was a lay reader. It has a Chinese-speaking, and an English-speaking, congregation. My mum gave me a gold cross that her mum had given her at confirmation. When I was really little, I used to go up the hill to Sunday School with my friends, and, when I was a bit older, to the teens' gatherings. It was more of a social thing, really, but we did discuss moral issues and Christian behaviour.

'Every year I was involved in some kind of play or production at Christmas. One year, for the teenage Sunday School performance, we did *The Lion, the Witch, and the Wardrobe*. I was the wicked witch because of my pale skin and blonde hair. Mum had a traditional Chinese qi pao dress with the high mandarin collar, white, with a black pattern through it. I wore that as a witch.

'My best friend from childhood, a girl who lived just down the road from us at the Tunghai campus, is now considering being ordained. And on the campus of the university, a Christian institution, there is a famous chapel designed to look like praying hands. I guess you could say I was surrounded by people of faith; but my parents, typical liberal intellectuals, always would challenge certain assumptions.

'In a way, I did as well. Morrison's theology didn't really sit well with me, though, and after a couple of years there, I became more cynical toward their form of indoctrination.'

For a time, Paul Harwood attempted to return to his Christian roots, but when it came to the point of complying with the vicar's wishes that he be confirmed, Paul baulked.

Katharine speaks from a rather remarkable objectivity:

'He's a very thoughtful person, my dad. He was brought up in a Church of England background, but he doesn't really believe in institutionalized religion. He used to spend quite a lot of time meditating and claims he is a Taoist, although he can be quite a depressive Taoist. He talks about how the world is getting worse and everything is going down the tubes, how people must get their act together or civilization as we know it won't survive. A typical kind of gloomy academic.

'My mum would bring my dad down to earth again. She is more of a realist in some respects. I don't know if I'm more like my dad or my mum. I think I've got a bit of both. I would class my mum as a lazy intellectual. She's not nearly so obsessed by some of the things my dad is. But she would hold her own in discussions with him and I think they counterbalanced each other very well.'

While Katharine thinks of her early childhood and teenage years as 'ordinary' and 'conventional', it is reasonable to assume that few would agree with her description of what is clearly a rather exotic youth. Living on a small Asian island, becoming bilingual at an age when most children are enchanted with discovering the alphabet, moving alone to a school continents away, and having parents who continually challenge their children's intellectual and moral development, is not all that usual. Neither is the deeply appreciated and fondly remembered relationship she had with Jon and Paul Harwood.

'Looking back at that period, I think our family was quite conventional in a sort of old-fashioned sense, where we would always sit down together for dinner every evening. We would have good, serious conversations, even when we were young teenagers sitting around the table with our parents. Mike and I were never allowed just to state an opinion; we had to provide reasons for our thinking. Moral considerations were important. We were challenged. But still it was very ordinary, very conventional, yet quite privileged in a sense.

'We were so fortunate. My parents' working hours averaged about fifteen to twenty hours a week in class, plus whatever preparation time was required at home. That meant they spent a lot of time with us when we were growing up. We were never latchkey kids. There always was somebody at home with us, someone willing to listen, someone who cared.

'My mum and I were close. But there were times when I was a teenager when we would bicker, and I would talk back and be generally rude. And I have this really clear memory of when it began, when I was about thirteen and being a really moody so-and-so, snapping and saying, "I hate you," and that sort of thing. I felt really bad about what I had done, and so that night I sat in bed and wrote a letter to my mum saying, "I'm really sorry I've been so awful. I don't know what's going on, but I just can't seem to control myself."

'I slipped the note under the door, and when I woke up the next morning there was a letter from my mum slipped under my bedroom door. It said, "It's perfectly normal, you have hormones racing through your body and of course you're going to be all uptight and confused and wondering what's happening to you. But you know we can always talk about these things. Let's be diplomatic and no more of this nonsense." I still have the letter, stored away in a box of my belongings.

'I have always confided in my mum in every stage of my growing-up process. I think our relationship, from the beginning, has made me strong.'

By the time Katharine was a teenager finishing her schooling at Morrison, the Harwood family had lived in Taiwan for many years beyond the intended two when they moved from England. An only child, Paul felt guilty about not returning home. Jan had lost her parents years earlier but still had strong ties to England. Each summer the family returned to England for a holiday, and each year leaving Durham behind became more difficult for Katharine's mother. Still, life was good in Taiwan, and both Paul and Jan were delighted with their teaching assignments and living arrangements.

'I tried to justify our staying in Taiwan to my mother-in-law,' Jan says. 'I recall saying, "Where in England could we be living where we didn't need a car, where we could walk ten minutes to our classrooms, where the kids can go to school on safe, private roads?"' Salaries were far from generous but provided for a comfortable lifestyle. 'We had help four hours a day six days a week. There's no way we could have domestic help like that in England on a teacher's salary!'

When she was sixteen, it was time for Katharine to leave Morrison and Taiwan for England and boarding school at Moira

House in Eastbourne. Although Katharine was well into her teens, she was still nervous about leaving home. Filled with apprehension, she approached her new school life cautiously.

'I was sixteen. It was very traumatic. My mum came back with me to England and we found a boarding school fairly close to my grandmother's younger sister, who lives on the south coast. My mum bought me a duvet, teacup and saucer, and all the things that were necessary for my little room at school. And left me there! It was a huge shock, so different from Morrison, where nobody smoked cigarettes, or drank alcohol, and where dancing – and nearly everything – was forbidden.

'So, I went from that, from an American missionary school, to a typical girls' boarding school in the United Kingdom. Loads of girls were sneakily smoking in the toilets, and sneaking out drinking after lights-out at night. They were just obsessed with boys and having these conversations – I couldn't believe it – about having sex! I was so shocked! Life there was a real eye-opener.

'I kind of naturally migrated toward all the girls in the school who weren't British, girls I felt more comfortable with. One was also from Taiwan, and there was a Japanese girl, two Korean girls, and a couple of girls from Hong Kong – just a mixed bag of Asian girls who became my closest friends. It took about a year for me to really feel settled in the school. I did, you know, have conversations with the English girls, but I felt much more comfortable and at home with my more conservative Asian friends.'

Teachers at Katharine's boarding school remember her as a good student, curious, responsive, and, one of them noted, willing to take a stand for something in which she believed. To complete her A levels, Katharine was required to take three subjects. She chose English literature and history. Her third choice was Chinese. Unfortunately, the school did not offer a Chinese course, but the examining board was willing to arrange tests for her if she would study for them privately. Her parents found a Chinese woman in the community who agreed to teach Katharine for a fee.

When she left boarding school for university, the study of Oriental languages was an obvious choice. So was selecting the same university her mother had attended, St Mary's College at Durham, where she completed a BA with honours in Chinese and Japanese.

Donald Starr, her university department head, has said of Katharine, 'She was very capable in Chinese and had an excellent cultural background because of her upbringing.'[1]

Life on a university campus was much more comfortable from the outset for Katharine, having been indoctrinated into Western ways at boarding school. Her studies went well for her, and her extreme naïveté was replaced by a more worldly outlook on life. A university contemporary has been quoted as noting, 'One felt that she had enjoyed a fairly cosseted existence on Taiwan, and Durham allowed her to spread her wings.'[2]

'Even though I was so far away, my relationship with my mum stayed strong while I was at university. Like the first time I slept with my boyfriend. I phoned her and said, "Mum, I've done it." She said, "I thought you were going to say something like that."

'Mum knew it was coming. I had called her midweek, and I usually called her on weekends from the university. I remember the conversation. I think it was a Wednesday. I said, "Is Daddy in the room?" and she said yes. So I said, "Just answer yes or no to my question. Should I go on the pill?" And she said, "Yes."

'I've never been afraid to go to her with anything, even if it was pretty embarrassing, like once I smoked a joint at a friend's house and got completely paranoid. It did really horrible things to me; I thought the TV was plotting against me. Mum was here, so I phoned her and said, "Mum, can you come and get me? I just smoked a joint and it really messed me up." She came straight away and said, "Oh, my God! You look green!"

'A lot of my friends, when I would tell them this sort of thing, would say, "Oh, I would never have told my mum something like that! I would never have told her when I had sex the first time or smoked a joint or whatever." And I would tell them, "But she's really cool about everything!" Of course, their answer was, "We want your mum!"'

When Katharine left university after graduating with an upper second-class degree, she applied for a teaching position in Japan through the Jet Programme, one popular with English-speaking university graduates from around the world. Katharine was accepted and thrilled at the prospect of returning to the Far East. Her teaching assignment was with middle-school children – quiet, shy teens eager to learn. The lifestyle and the work suited her.

Katharine's school was in a picturesque, remote mountainous village in the Hiroshima prefecture, miles away from the city essentially cremated by the first atomic bomb ever dropped on an enemy. Life in her village was a dramatic change from anything she had experienced previously, and she found it as distant in feeling as the miles that separated it from Hiroshima.

Katharine's first visit to the restored city was emotionally disturbing.

'It's so moving. I don't know what I expected of Hiroshima. It is a bustling modern city now, no different from any other, until you go to the Peace Memorial Park. One building was left intact, standing near ground zero. They haven't done a thing to it, and it's just an empty shell of a building. It has an arched dome, held up by metal rods. The steel is still standing, and a few bits of the brick, then the uprights. And, of course, there's the museum. The images, picturing what had happened there – you just can't get them out of your mind. Not ever. Being there has to have an impact on you. I thought of the children, like those I was teaching every day. Like those who died here.

'There aren't many people left alive in Japan now who are old enough to remember, but there are some. I met elders in our village who talked about how people would trek for miles into the mountains to try to escape from the radiation. Some were moved out of the city to recuperate in the countryside, where there was very little damage. Their memories are still vivid.'

One is compelled to wonder whether Katharine's experience at Hiroshima's Peace Memorial Park had a bearing on the decision she made the weekend following receipt of the Koza message, to ask her if those disturbing images influenced her attempt to stop a war.

'I suppose they must have, although I never really thought about it in that way when I made my decision. I was thinking the build-up to the war was very hasty, and it was worrying – and wrong. And I was, in fact, concerned about bombs falling on innocent civilians, thinking there had to be a better way.'

In the summer of 1999, Katharine left the village in Japan's mountains to return to England. Her two-year teaching commitment had been a grand experience, but it was time now to explore new and, perhaps, more exciting career options. Ideally, she would find something that would utilize her excellent language skills.

That something appeared unexpectedly in the form of a discreet advertisement for translators at GCHQ. Katharine knew next to nothing about the agency, the mysterious Government Communication Headquarters, which made the advertisement that much more enticing. The employment application process was lengthy, thorough, and involved proficiency testing in her area of linguistic concentration. While she plodded through the inevitable bureaucratic maze and seemingly endless red tape, Katharine worked at a variety of temporary assignments. Eventually, finally, she was notified of her acceptance.

On 22 January 2001, Katharine Harwood became a British intelligence officer, her assignment translating Mandarin at GCHQ in Cheltenham. She was twenty-six.

By the time Katharine signed her employment agreement, with its Official Secrets Act provisions, her cultural being was a colourful, simmering synthesis of a somewhat tranquil West and a vibrant East. Its elements were a British heritage and schooling, Chinese life experience, American education at Morrison Academy, and later a Japanese experience that included the Peace Memorial Park. It made her the epitome of a 'third-culture kid,' a child who, in a sense, created her own culture, an admixture of that which she inherited and that to which she was exposed.

Katharine's way of speaking reflects this unique synthesis. The toddler who first went to Taiwan had a distinct British accent, even at three years. Her fluent Chinese, confidently spoken a remarkably short time after moving to Taiwan, was almost without foreign inflection. Later, her British accent vanished in the American environment at Morrison, only to return full strength soon after she began her studies at boarding school.

With language goes thought, and it seems clear that coalescing and separating linguistic experiences have influenced her thinking over the years. They have helped create a personal code of life that is paradoxically diverse and focused.

Within the psyche of the grown-up Katharine is an inviolable personal ethic, perhaps initially codified at Morrison, or perhaps earlier around the Harwood dinner table. Listed specifically in her mental book of rules are fairness and justice and truth — whether it's telling Mum about illegal smoking or confessing high crime to Inspector Tintin. The self-protecting 'white lie' concerning her status at GCHQ following her arrest bothers her still. Overseeing the rule book is the conscience Katharine has called 'a nuisance'." As a result, she is ferociously honest.

A rather disarming statement made by the young woman arrested for leaking Frank Koza's message was destined to become the media's sound bite of choice, the headline of dozens of news stories — a motto of sorts. The media unabashedly loved it and still do.

'I have only ever followed my conscience.'

PART IV

THE LEGAL CASE

CHAPTER 11: The Blonde Who Dropped the Bombshell

Katharine Gun, a former GCHQ civil servant, today has been charged with offences under the Official Secrets Act relating to public interest disclosures allegedly made in the run-up to the Iraq War.

Note to editors: This case is likely to put the legality of the Iraq War on trial.

— From a 13 November 2003 Liberty press release

F OR EIGHT MONTHS, Katharine Gun hoped the government would decide not to charge her for the crime to which she had confessed. If the case against her were dropped, the public — and even most of her colleagues in the secret service — would never learn that it was she who revealed the NSA message. After so many months, the prospect of being charged had seemed to fade. Surely, she told herself, again and again, the government would have acted by now if it intended to do so.

The 12 November call from Liberty informing Katharine that she would be charged the following day was a devastating blow. It left her trembling and breathless in a fog of disbelief and denial. As much as she should have been prepared, the reality of what was happening was crushing. Thoughts of having her name in headlines, of seeing herself on television news, made her physically ill. Among the montage of mental images were friends, neighbours, former intelligence colleagues, class-mates at Birmingham – all of whom would be shocked. Gone was the fantasy of simply vanishing 'under the rug' to live the rest of her life in peace. The rug had been pulled out from under her.

Katharine had just one day to prepare for what she knew would be a media onslaught following her court appearance and announcement of the charge against her. With a subdued Yasar, she made detailed plans to elude an eager press. There was little rest that night, the worst she had experienced since her arrest.

On 13 November 2003, Metropolitan Police Special Branch officers made their formal charge at Cheltenham Police Station. In a brief, one paragraph indictment, Katharine Teresa Gun was charged with violation of Section 1(1) of the Official Secrets Act of 1989.[1] The accused was bailed to appear at Bow Street Magistrates Court on 27 November. It was over in a matter of minutes.

Liberty immediately issued a press release announcing that it was acting for Katharine Gun, 'a former GCHQ civil servant who has today been charged with offences under the Official Secrets Act'. Those offences, said Liberty, 'related to public interest disclosures allegedly made in the run-up to the Iraq War'.

Katharine made a statement on her own behalf. It would receive worldwide attention (or almost): 'I have been charged with offences under the Official Secrets Act. Any disclosures that may have been made were justified on the following grounds: because they exposed serious illegality and wrongdoing on the part of the US government who attempted to subvert our own security services, and to prevent wide-scale death and casualties among ordinary Iraqi people and UK forces in the course of an illegal war. No one has suggested (nor could they) that any payment was sought or given for any alleged dis-closures. I have only ever followed my conscience.'

Katharine could not imagine, at the time she made her statement, the lasting relevancy of her exposing 'serious illegality and wrongdoing on the part of the US government'. Four years later, people around the globe were still debating the legality of the war and wrongdoing in support of its initiation – politically and ethically still hot topics. More than a few members of the US Congress who had given George Bush a green light to attack were regretting that decision and questioning the war's legality. As the election year of 2008 approached, candidates of both major parties pointed Iraq War fingers at each other, accusing, explaining, reacting. Casualties, even though their numbers decreased following the Bush administration's military 'surge', were regrettably still a tragic fact of everyday life. They were impossible to ignore, despite a thoughtful government's shielding the public from the discouraging sight of those flag-draped coffins returning from the war zone.

In her statement, Katharine Gun had fired a potent shot and hit her target square on. At the time, however, the words that attracted most media attention were these: 'I have only ever followed my conscience.'

By now, Yvonne Ridley had left London to work in Qatar for Al Jazeera as a senior editor to help launch its English website. The day Katharine was charged had special meaning for her.

'Out of the blue, I was fired from my job and told I was a "threat to national security and the beautiful state of Qatar". I always remember that phrase with a smile,' she says. 'I was informed at around ten o'clock at night on exactly the same day – and the corresponding GMT time – that Katharine was charged. Coincidence? Who knows?'

As predicted, a tense game of hide-and-seek followed news of Katharine's court appearance. 'I knew my name would come out and everything would change,' Katharine says. 'I didn't think they would tell my address, didn't think that it would appear in the newspapers. But in the end, it didn't matter, because the tabloids were determined to find us. They came searching, scouring the neighbourhood, looking everywhere, asking questions.' For a full week the press continued its pursuit, 'desperately trying to find' the Guns.

The mainstream press covered the story upfront. Typical headlines were, 'GCHQ whistle blower charged', and 'Ex-GCHQ officer preventing war'. It was a journalistic field day. The identity of the young woman who tried to nix the war plans of a British prime minister and a US president was now revealed to the world.

'Ms Gun, a GCHQ translator,' wrote the *Guardian* on 14 November, 'was arrested in March – more than eight months ago – at a time when it was reported that America's National Security Agency, the US equivalent of GCHQ, was conducting a "dirty tricks" operation.' The story also noted that Katharine had 'only ever followed my conscience'.

Tabloid photographers were after 'lifestyle' pictures, the kind of images sought in high-profile criminal cases – on a 'pictorial fishing exercise', says Katharine. Reporters went to Yasar's brother, the only person in the local directory named Gun. They quickly surmised that since Katharine wasn't seen with her 'husband', the young marriage had not survived the wife's perfidy, and she was in hiding, alone. In fact, Katharine had escaped to her grandmother in Yorkshire, and Yasar was hiding out with friends – their plan for eluding the paparazzi a success.

'I don't think my grandma realized at the time how serious it was, but my great-aunt heard it on the news and lay awake every night worrying, as I did. I felt frightened and powerless.' Katharine's parents shared those feelings, wanting to help, yet knowing that all they could offer at the moment was 'a shoulder to cry on', she says. 'Dad, the worrier, managed to keep a typically British stiff upper lip – you know, "keep your chin up, and we'll get through this".' Contacted by telephone in Taiwan, Jan Harwood gave a brief statement to the press. Her daughter was not a criminal.

Katharine Gun was now famous – or infamous, depending. On 27 November, Katharine appeared at London's Bow

Street court in what was a legal administrative formality. She confirmed her name and address. Liberty lawyers were at her side. Senior district judge Timothy Workman granted unconditional bail and set 19 January for the defendant's next appearance at Bow Street. At that time, a magistrate would decide whether to send the case to a Crown court.

Outside, Liberty read a statement from Katharine: 'I have today indicated to the court that I intend to plead not guilty to the charge that I face under the Official Secrets Act. I will defend the charge against me on the basis that my actions were necessary to prevent an illegal war in which thousands of Iraqi citizens and British soldiers would be killed or maimed.'

Katharine repeated her earlier statement about payment and conscience, adding that she had been 'heartened by the many messages of support and encouragement . . . received from Britain and around the world'.

On 18 January, the day before Katharine would hear the lower court's decision, the *Observer* reviewed the NSA operation for its readers – just in case anyone had forgotten what all the fuss was about.

'The document urged Britain to join in a dirty-tricks operation,' reminded the newspaper. It also predicted that a trial against Katharine Gun 'will call into question the legality of the war', adding that 'Most experts in international law believed then that intervention would be illegal. Many still do.'

It would be misleading to imply that all media reports about the case were supportive. There were those that castigated Katharine and found what she had done to be traitorous and abysmal. They reflected passionately negative views abroad in the land. Some were from intelligence and government circles, where fervent hope simmered in various protective cauldrons that the former GCHQ translator would get what she deserved – a goodly amount of time behind bars.

The lower court's decision came quickly and was exactly what was anticipated. After all, the Crown had had more than eight months to study its case. Thus, on 19 January 2004,

Katharine Gun was committed for trial at the Old Bailey for violation of the Official Secrets Act. As before, the hearing was expected to be little more than the formality of binding Katharine over to the high court; however, there was a significant hitch. Her former employer was determined to keep Katharine quiet. Even with regard to working with counsel.

'GCHQ has imposed a blanket restriction on the ability of Katharine Gun to give instructions to her lawyers,' Liberty solicitor Ben Emmerson complained. The ultra secret agency had banned its former employee from saying anything to her lawyers about her work, a gag order Emmerson vowed to get lifted as soon as possible. He did so, but not before there was a great deal of nattering about the fairness of refusing a client full access to her counsel.[2]

Katharine was scheduled to appear at the Old Bailey on 16 February. At this point, there were predictions that she would go on trial at the historic court sometime in the autumn.

Finally, the US media took at least a modicum of interest in the Gun case; apparently, it was now considered safe to do so. Frank Koza's message had been e-mailed nearly a year ago, and there were sufficient new Iraq-related issues to worry the general public. The reason for the media's sudden (if limited) interest in what was happening in England was a statement signed by a group of American celebrities, names that would make news whatever – or whomever – they were supporting.

During the weekend, just before Katharine's Monday appearance in court, Hollywood actors Sean Penn, Danny Glover and Martin Sheen, civil rights leader Jesse Jackson, feminist Gloria Steinem, famed whistle-blower Daniel Ellsberg, Newspaper Guild president Linda Foley (as an individual, she stressed), and prominent others issued a press release honouring Katharine Gun and urging that the US media inform the public about her case. They asked elected officials to express their concern to the British government. It was an extraordinary petition, given the preponderance of pro-war sentiment in the United States at the time.

Because of the celebrity status of the document's signatories, at least a few Americans began to take note of the NSA spy scandal and the young woman who had revealed it. A few bits and pieces appeared in various media, but not enough to enlighten the public as a whole. And some who did take note no doubt wondered. Should the words of Sean Penn and liberal pals of that ilk be dismissed out of hand, or was there something of substance going on here?

New York Times columnist Bob Herbert thought there was. He wrote on 19 January, the day Katharine was committed to trial at the Old Bailey, 'Katharine Gun has a much better grasp of the true spirit of democracy than Tony Blair. So, naturally, it's Katharine Gun who's being punished.'

Herbert pulled no journalistic punches. 'We are not talking about a big-time criminal here . . . someone who would undermine the democratic principles that George W. Bush and Tony Blair babble about so incessantly, and self-righteously, even as they are trampling on them,' wrote Herbert.

Colourful, outspoken, the late Texas columnist Molly Ivins took up the cause and, with her usual bite and passion, wrote, 'Friends of liberty, raise hell! To the barricades, or at least to the post office and the e-mails.' She urged her readers to contact the British Embassy or the Institute for Public Accuracy on Katharine's behalf. 'It is not a good idea,' she said, 'to set things up so that people get punished for telling the truth – or even re-elected for telling lies.'[3]

From 12 November onwards, once the shock of being charged and becoming a media phenomenon had lessened, Liberty's Tabard Street office and the legal experts who resided there became Katharine's life. The few available quiet moments she spent in solitude with Yasar, except for rare hours with a handful of loyal friends. She no longer worried about photographers, no longer hid from public notice. She simply had no time for all of that. There was work to be done if she was to avoid years in prison.

It was inevitable that the press would now come to call

Katharine Gun 'the blonde who dropped the bombshell on Tony Blair.' Increasingly, his government was being pictured as having been led into egregious wrong doing by a skinny cowboy in an oversized Stetson, an image sharpened by the media's attention to Katharine's deed and its impact on Downing Street.

The blonde had indeed dropped a bombshell on Tony Blair. But that same bomb had exploded on George W. Bush, the only difference being that he failed to notice.

CHAPTER 12: Deportation Revisited

I always seem to be writing to you in a bit of a state. I wish that I could be cheerful and have good news for you.[1]

— Katharine Gun

KATHARINE GUN WAS not the only one dropping bombshells. The British government had one of its own, targeting not Katharine but her husband. This is not to say that what they did, or tried to do, was illegal or prejudicial. Having said that, one can be excused for wondering about the timing of it all. Recently charged with a serious crime against the people of the United Kingdom, Katharine suddenly found herself in another conflict with the law.

She begins, on a cold January day: 'At lunchtime, as was true every week, Yasar had to go to the police station to sign a piece of paper for immigration purposes. We knew after the first deportation attempt, two weeks following our marriage, that his status was still insecure, but we didn't know just how insecure. We found out soon enough.

'Because it was so cold, I waited in the car outside the station. Yasar seemed to be taking his time. Suddenly, two young girls came out of the station and asked, "Are you waiting for your husband?" I said that I was, and they said, "He's been taken into the cells by the police."

'Terrified, I jumped out of the car and dashed into the police station. It had been less than ten minutes since he left me, but there was no trace of him in the reception area. I asked the lady officer behind the desk what was going on. She cheerfully responded, "Your husband is going back to Turkey." I almost shouted at her, "How can you say that? He's my husband! You can't take him away!" All she could say was, "It's out of our control; this is an immigration matter."

'I tried to see Yasar, but the officer wouldn't let me. She showed me his deportation papers, and there it stated, quite clearly, that he was booked on a flight to Turkey scheduled the following day.

'I left the station weeping and cried the whole way home. Luckily, my dad was staying with us, as he had a Chinese New Year teaching break from his Taiwan university. I opened the door and sobbed, "They've taken him again." He looked aghast. "The bastards!" he said.

'I knew I had to do something in a hurry. We'd chosen a new lawyer to act on Yasar's behalf after the first one seemed to do very little. This woman, extremely considerate and efficient, promised to do what she could. Next, I called my member of Parliament, Mr Nigel Jones, who was a Liberal Democrat. His was the only party that officially opposed the war in Iraq. He was in a meeting in London, but his assistant said she would beep him urgently. I was frantic, but I kept trying, calling anyone I could think of who might be able to help.

'Nigel Jones managed to corner a minister for home affairs, Beverley Hughes. He suggested that to deport Yasar at this time would look like state bullying, as I had been charged two months earlier. She seemed to agree. Our lawyer argued that since my passport had been taken away during my legal proceedings, I would be unable to join him if he were sent back to Turkey. This could be considered a breach of our basic human right to a family life. I knew we had a case, but was terrified that the immigration officers would fail to get news of what was happening in time to stop the deportation process.

'By now, I still hadn't spoken to Yasar, and it was getting frighteningly late. Eventually, that evening I managed to speak to him on the phone. I reassured him that we were doing everything possible to stop his deportation. I tried not to cry, tried to sound strong and encouraging. But he seemed resigned to the inevitable. It was heartbreaking.

'The next day I rushed down to the police station with fresh clothes, hoping that the immigration officers had been informed of efforts to stop the deportation, and that my husband would be let go. Perhaps he already was free! But when I arrived, the police officer in charge told me that he was already on his way to Heathrow Airport.

'I rushed home and began making frantic calls. Around eleven, Yasar rang from the departure lounge of the airport. He was devastated, fully believing the battle was lost, not knowing when we would ever see each other again. It could be years.

'He said he'd asked to call me before he left Cheltenham in the immigration van, but they wouldn't let him. I wanted to scream, thinking the system unbelievably callous. They at least could have let us say goodbye. I hadn't seen Yasar since he got out of our car the previous day; we hadn't hugged or kissed. Was this going to be farewell? We ended the conversation in tears. My heart was in my mouth, why hadn't word got through yet?

'For the next several hours I was in a state of panic. And then, Yasar called from his mobile! He was on his way to a detention centre in Oxford. An enormous relief – at least he wasn't on a flight to Turkey. After three days of being held in detention, he was released and given six months' leave to remain in the United Kingdom. From what I could gather afterwards, Ms Hughes was in direct touch with immigration officials at the airport and told them not to put my husband on the flight.

'From being two ordinary people, newly married, looking forward to a future together, we were now two not-very-ordinary people. I had been very much in the news and was likely to be there for some time to come. Both of us, for different reasons, had been behind bars. We were two young people whose future was, at best, uncertain.'

CHAPTER 13: The Prosecution and the Defence Prepare for Court

The defendant admits that she disclosed the email which is the subject of this indictment to another person, and that she did so intending that its contents would be put into the public domain . . . The defence case is that she was lawfully entitled to make the disclosure.

– from the Advance Notice of Defence Statement

She claims 'the defense of necessity,' that her leak was required 'to expose serious wrongdoing on the part of the US government,' and 'to prevent an illegal war in which thousands would be killed.' Her trial will rehash the war's legality – still a touchy subject, especially since no Iraqi weapons of mass destruction have been found.[1]

– J. F. O. McAllister

KEEN ATTENTION NOW focused on the young Englishwoman facing trial on charges of high crime committed in an attempt to stop a war. Ahead of her was the likelihood of years in prison. As preparation for her trial at the historic Old Bailey neared, speculation about what would happen to the attractive young defendant increasingly became the subject of public debate and private discussion. The woman and the crime fascinated an international audience, a drama playing out against the backdrop of an unpopular war. A modern-day Jeanne d'Arc, said some.

It is safe to say that a great many who watched the legal drama in London felt as did *Time* writer McAllister, who titled his report, 'A smoking gun puts the war on trial'. It was not the woman, but the war that belonged in the defendant's dock. The case was not and had never been about Katharine Gun, but always about the war's legality.

Adding to the prevailing rumours and speculation circulating across the country was talk that Crown prosecutors were becoming nervous about Katharine. Press photos pictured a defendant who was annoyingly young and appealing, with the seemingly innocent countenance of a youngster in need of protection – an image that might influence a jury. It was not difficult to believe she was acting solely as a matter of conscience.

If prosecutors were nervous, Tony Blair and his inner circle must have been as well. In a worst-case scenario, the Crown's high-powered legal team had only a trial to lose. Downing Street had far more at stake. Against the war from the beginning, the British were living in a climate of increasing displeasure with what was happening and not happening in Iraq. Coalition soldiers were dying, as predicted by the GCHQ translator who tried to stop the war. No weapons of mass destruction had been found, and there was suspicion, more so than in the United States, that they likely did not exist. Debate over allegations that the government had deliberately manipulated intelligence in support of the war had not been put to rest by Lord Hutton's finding a month earlier that those allegations were unfounded. The ugly word 'whitewash' continued to surface.

In the very worst case for the prime minister, Gun could become a lightning rod for anti-war protests, win or lose. If she were convicted, she could become a martyr of sorts; if freed, she could become a huge source of embarrassment to the government. Further, the very integrity of the Official Secrets Act would be challenged.

Finally, and most dangerous, was that the upcoming trial would bring even more attention to questions about the war's legality, questions inevitably leading to speculation about the attorney general's advice to Blair. Abundant media interest about the case was exacerbating an already politically precarious situation at Downing Street.

One pithy remark summed up what so many were now thinking, 'Katharine Gun will not go quietly.'[2] Whatever happened, the political noise could be deafening.

Although the indictment read *The Queen v. Katharine Teresa Gun*, Katharine was being prosecuted by the Crown Prosecution Service (CPS) on behalf of the public, not the Queen, and not the government – as is true in all criminal indictments in the United Kingdom.

To proceed to trial, Katharine's prosecutors had to be convinced that their case likely was winnable, a level of confidence required by provisions of the Code for Crown Prosecutors. The code mandates an 'evidential test' as the first stage in creating that confidence. With regard to the case now receiving so much attention, Katharine's prosecutors had little difficulty in passing the test – at least at the outset. It specifically states that prosecutors must be satisfied that their evidence will provide a 'realistic prospect of conviction'. They certainly had that. The burden of proof required was 'beyond reasonable doubt' (and there seemed little room for doubt), with a jury expected to try to reach a unanimous verdict. In the unlikely event that unanimity was not possible, the court would accept a verdict agreed by at least ten of the twelve jurors. Winnable? Yes.

Further, stipulates the code, prosecutors are required to consider what the defence case will be and how it will affect the prosecution's case. UK law provides that they must do this last bit of legal speculation without benefit of questioning the defendant in advance of prosecution, without 'precognition'. But prosecutors knew, or thought they knew, everything necessary to defeat her not-guilty plea. On legal balance, the scale seemed weighted in favour of the prosecution. Technically, their case should withstand Katharine's challenge. Technically.

Yet another requirement instructs Crown prosecutors to consider whether the evidence can be used and is reliable. Certainly, their evidence was 'usable', and certainly it was reliable to the point of being inviolable.

The second stage in determining whether to prosecute is the public interest test. The CPS will start or continue when the case has passed both tests. The answer was obvious: to bring to justice someone who threatened the security of the nation as blatantly as had Katharine would certainly be in the public interest.

Thus, while Katharine's team devoted itself to mounting a 'defence of necessity/duress', the prosecution already had the answer to combat that defence, with seemingly every advantage. One, Katharine Gun was covered by the Official Secrets Act; two, she admitted to having committed a crime in violation of that Act. A fatal one-two punch.

Katharine's defence of 'necessity' was founded on 'iffy' and risky grounds. It has a troubled history and is rarely successful. It makes demands that are difficult to prove, a legal rationale difficult to justify. In the case of David Shayler, the defendant lost his final argument.[3] Yet the judge, Lord Woolf, ruled that a defence of necessity might (but only might) be used in extreme cases, such as the imminent protection of lives.[4]

A seemingly more obvious defence, that Katharine had acted in the public interest, is not permitted under British law – specifically prohibited, in fact, by the Official Secrets Act as revised in 1989. The OSA now states expressly that there will be no public interest defence. No defendant can claim in court that he or she broke the law in the national interest. Period.

A defence of necessity, says Liberty solicitor James Welch, goes beyond the concept of public interest. 'The hurdle is much higher. A person relying on the defence needs to show that he/she acted to avoid serious injury or death to him/herself or others.' Pleading necessity, a defendant must prove that the single available response to a situation of overwhelming urgency necessitated breaking the law.

Precedent makes it clear that necessity should be denied as a general defence.[5] Needing an automobile to drive the children to school does not allow a parent to steal a car. Even being hungry is not a defence for hitting the bakery on a dark night. There are other resolutions available in these cases. What is required is the existence of an urgent and profound threat to life for self or others and a reaction to it that is proportionate. Otherwise, legal pundits have observed, anarchy could result, with law and order no longer the rule of civilized society.

In Katharine's case, 'duress' was included in her defence. The distinction between the two is that necessity applies to circumstances arising naturally, whereas duress applies to circumstances arising from an overpowering human source. Katharine, Liberty held, was entitled to break the law because acts of the US and UK governments posed imminent danger to human lives. Clear enough, but very difficult to prove given that there were, or should have been, other avenues open to her.

The higher hurdle identified by Welch was in Liberty's Tabard Street offices as convicted whistle-blower David Shayler was saying four days before Katharine's Old Bailey appearance, 'The 1989 Official Secrets Act remains a cancer in the body politic.'[6]

Following the Crown's high-profile, failed 1985 OSA case against whistle-blower Clive Ponting, revision of the act in 1989 tightened the original. Civil servant Ponting leaked information about the sinking of the Argentine ship the *General Belgrano* during the Falklands War. Hundreds of lives were lost in a misadventure because, Ponting claimed, ministers misled the public into thinking the *Belgrano* was threatening British lives.

A source considered reliable told the authors that there are still two schools of thought about Ponting, a case some compare to Katharine's. The *Belgrano* was, this British citizen says, carrying weapons and was not, as Ponting insisted, innocently sailing away from the battle zone.

Whatever the truth, Ponting won his case.

Other OSA losses led to the new, tougher attitude about whistle-blowing in the name of public good, an attitude that buttressed the Crown's case against Katharine. There have been some notable prosecution successes since enactment of the revision, including jailing of both Shayler and MI6 officer Richard Tomlinson, the first for passing intelligence service information to a journalist and the second for passing secrets to an Australian publisher. For Katharine's team, Ponting was a cause for hope; Shayler and Tomlinson were a cause for concern.

Violation of the Official Secrets Act is one of the crimes the CPS takes to the attorney general for concurrence once the decision to prosecute is made. His support was to be expected. Katharine's crime fitted the revised Official Secrets Act provisions perfectly.

Despite all that was in their favour, there was that simmering prosecutorial nervousness based on factors other than those that were technical – the war and the woman. However, with knowledge of the game, the rules, and the players, the decision to proceed with plans to try Katharine was holding, or seemed to be. And then a new rumour began to circulate: Perhaps the Crown was changing its mind, was considering dropping the case. There were two questions: Why? And who might be involved in that change of mind or, perhaps, heart?

It would have been egregiously unethical – and illegal to boot – for a worried Blair government to put pressure on Crown prosecutors to end the whole sorry business at this point. Government has no role in a decision to prosecute, made by the Crown Prosecution Service alone – although, as noted, in certain cases the attorney general must concur. (Blair would make this patently clear the following day.) The reality of independence is significant, and one fiercely protected by the

CPS. No ministerial interference, no influence peddling by politicians at any level or of any distinction.

It is true that director of prosecutions Ken Macdonald, QC, a veteran of twenty-five years of criminal law practice, reports to the attorney general, who is a political appointee of the prime minister. Said Macdonald following his fall 2003 appointment, 'A transparent, fair and effective prosecuting authority is one of the hallmarks of a great liberal democracy. This is our aim.'[7]

After Katharine Gun faced her accusers in the Old Bailey, one wonders if there might have been some doubting eyebrows quietly raised about independence and transparency, never mind that both are guaranteed not only by law, but also by process. It may or may not have been a coincidence in timing when, a week after that confrontation, Lord Goldsmith told the House of Lords: 'My Lords, I want to start by making one thing clear. I want to leave the House and the people of this country in no doubt. I stand for the independence of the Crown Prosecution Service. No one will challenge that while I am Her Majesty's Attorney-General.'[8]

Americans understand the concept of independent 'special' prosecution in high-level, controversial cases like that of President Bill Clinton. But in the United States, this avenue of dealing with alleged criminal activity is rarely taken and is in response to extraordinary political pressure. In the United Kingdom, it is the only avenue.

Time was running out. The Queen versus Katharine Gun could be distilled to its essentials: With her confession in hand, CPS prosecutors had all the evidence they needed to prevail in their case against Katharine Gun; with her defence, Katharine had to prove her act met the strict requirements of the law, that it was intended to prevent an illegal war and the loss of lives. That it was necessary.

As both sides were wrapping up their cases and figuring their odds for success, Katharine's team concentrated on Blair's unconvincing assurance that the pre-emptive strike against Iraq was legal, that it was in full accord with international agreements to which the United Kingdom was a signatory.

It was on 17 March 2003, some two weeks after Katharine's arrest and the failure of the UNSC second resolution, that Attorney General Lord Goldsmith gave Parliament a brief statement of opinion on the war's legality. Since that time, the prime minister repeatedly reaffirmed the reliability of Goldsmith's unequivocal green light to attack. But in the modest confines of Liberty's offices, as elsewhere in London, there were suspicions about a blinking yellow. Perhaps the 17 March opinion replaced an earlier and more cautious consideration of legal implications involved in a pre-emptive strike.

Perhaps.

In Taiwan, Jan Harwood was contacted and asked to prepare two statements for the media – one expressing disappointment over her daughter's defeat in court, the other expressing joy over her success. It would save time and effort, she was told. She complied.

At the last minute, at noon the day before what would prove to be a historic confrontation at the Old Bailey, Liberty sent prosecutors an Advance Notice of Defence Statement, with a specific request for certain documents to be supplied by the prosecution, documents that supposedly did not exist.

It was a brilliant move and one that changed the game – and odds – entirely.

PART V

AFTERMATH

CHAPTER 14: A Historic Collapse at the Old Bailey

A trial would also have been a forum on the legality of American espionage aimed at influencing the six undecided nations' votes.[1]

– Liberty statement, 25 February 2004

Dropping the charges will avoid severe government embarrassment. There is little doubt that Ms Gun, and her legal advisers, would have been bound to put the legality of military action in Iraq at the very centre of their defence. It is even possible that the full text of the attorney general's advice to the cabinet might have been published at last.

– Sir Menzies Campbell, upon the collapse of the Gun trial

THE BOLD, BRILLIANT move conceived at the last minute by Katharine Gun's Liberty defence team took form in a specific request included in an Advance Notice of Defence Statement to be sent to Crown prosecutors. It would demand that the prosecution disclose 'any record, memorandum, or legal opinion or advice tending to support the defendant's honest and reasonable belief that it was (or had been) the view of the UK government that going to war against

Iraq without a second UN Security Council resolution would be contrary to international law.'[2]

Contrary to international law? This was not the official line. The government had claimed all along that war against Iraq without a second UNSC resolution was viewed as legal.

The statement in its entirety expands upon Katharine's belief that her country would not enter a war illegally, that it would not join in a conflict against Iraq without that authorizing resolution. Thus, she attempted to stop a war by destroying its potential trigger mechanism: the second resolution that would make war legal.

'She believed the joint negotiating position of the United States and the United Kingdom would be undermined by the disclosure [of the Koza message], because the email revealed the existence of an operation being conducted by the United States National Security Agency, using means which were unlawful and contrary to international law . . . with a view to manipulating the vote of the UN Security Council on a second resolution.'[3]

Katharine's motives, her 'honest and reasonable beliefs', had been made public time and again and were nothing new. They were all a part of her defence of 'necessity/duress of circumstances'. What was new was the very specific request seeking disclosure of unpublished advice on the legality of war without the sanction of a second resolution, an opinion tenaciously held confidential by the prime minister. The implication was that there were conflicting opinions given – one, made public, supporting Blair's insistence that the war was legal; another, kept secret, raising significant questions about that insistence.

'The defence believes that the advice given by the Foreign Office Legal Adviser expressed serious doubts about the legality (in international law) of committing British troops in the absence of a second resolution,' reads the statement.[4] Much of what follows in the statement is obscured by heavy black lines, specifics lost to a censor's pen.

It is assumed that the Foreign Office legal adviser referred to here is Elizabeth Wilmshurst, who resigned over the attorney general's about-face on the war's legality. Even without a government-censored paragraph, Wilmshurst's letter of resignation makes clear that there was more than one opinion delivered to the prime minister.

For months, Blair had refused to bend to increasing pressure for disclosure of the attorney general's initial opinion, insisting it would be inappropriate to share it with the public. Instead, he repeatedly referred to Lord Goldsmith's written statement given to Parliament ten days following the 'confidential' opinion delivered to him. On occasion, he declared that advice of this nature was privileged and always kept private.

The final section of the advance notice given to prosecutors by the Liberty team articulated the defence posture with regard to continuance of the case against Katharine Gun. Failure to comply with the defence demand would be considered 'an abuse of process for the prosecution to proceed, since disclosure of the material is necessary to secure a fair trial'.[5]

It is not unreasonable to conclude that the defence placed disclosure of the requested information, and the success or failure of the Crown's case, on Blair's political doorstep. Equally reasonably, one might conclude differently. And Blair would later make abundantly clear in statements to the press that he was not involved in the decision to prosecute, or not to prosecute, Katharine Gun.

The defence document was delivered to the Crown Prosecution Service on Tuesday. Katharine would appear before the judge at the Old Bailey on Wednesday. The flurry of calls among the prosecutors, the director of prosecutions, the foreign secretary, and others late that Tuesday afternoon is easy to imagine. It is identification of the 'others' that intrigues the mind.

The defence stage was set for the following day's drama – until Tuesday evening, when a telephone call came to Liberty from Crown prosecutors. The drama would have a single act, a single scene. Unless someone had a change of mind when the curtain rose.

Katharine tells the story from her perspective: 'I was nervous and shaking. Last week, out of the blue, the *Guardian* reported a rumour that the prosecution might drop the charges against me. When I read the article, I was thrilled to think it could possibly happen! Still, it struck me that if the rumour were true, the prosecution would have notified us. And my husband, ever cautious, counselled me not to count my chickens before they hatched. After all these months of preparing for trial, why would they suddenly decide to let me go?

'Because of the rumour, and because I was going to the Old Bailey, I knew media attention would be focused on me, no matter what happened. I felt I needed a nice new outfit for the occasion. So, that weekend I asked one of my friends, who was still working at GCHQ and living at Cheltenham, to help me search for a new suit. We found one I liked and I bought it. Sounds silly, I suppose, but buying a new outfit helped me face the Old Bailey.

'I learned the night before going to the courthouse that the rumour was true. They were going to drop charges! I was at Liberty talking about how we would organize, about what we would do the following day at court. It was while this was going on that James Welch got a phone call from the prosecution saying that they were offering no evidence. There would be no trial! We were absolutely bowled over. Here we were in Liberty's offices, leaping with joy and hugging everybody, and then Shami [the Liberty director, Shami Chakrabarti] said, "We've got to celebrate! We must go out to dinner!" So that evening, we all went to a Turkish restaurant not far from where Liberty is based. I was so excited and nervous that I really didn't have much of an appetite, even though it was delicious food. That night I went to bed knowing they planned to drop the charges against me. For the first time in almost a year, I fell asleep without the thought of prison rattling around in my brain.

'Normally, I would go up to London the day before my court hearings, so that I wouldn't have to travel to court early in the morning. This is all very funny, looking back now, because on the occasions that I'd been to court, I'd stayed with people that I knew from GCHQ. I wonder what the higher-ups would think about staff harbouring Katharine Gun!

'This time I was staying with one of my GCHQ friends who was training in another language and temporarily based in London, where the government had provided her with a very nice two-bedroom apartment. I remember so clearly getting up that morning and dressing in my nice new suit and feeling really very nervous. My friend had to go to her language class as usual, so we said goodbye at the door. She gave me a hug, wished me good luck, and off I went.

'I made my way down from the North London apartment to Liberty's offices, where I met Shami and James and everybody. We got a cab to the courthouse, and when we arrived there were people watching for us – photographers, but I wasn't mobbed. We met my barrister, Ben Emmerson, who was waiting by the front door. My stomach was churning. I was counting my chickens, but they were yet to hatch.

'The Old Bailey is a huge, huge building, completely different from the older magistrate courts. In spite of its name, the Old Bailey is a new building and doesn't feel like a court at all. You walk up these enormous staircases to various courtrooms. We went through a security check, then climbed the stairs to the courtroom where we were meant to be. We were early and went into a café to wait, surrounded by lawyers and barristers wearing wigs and robes. It was difficult to appreciate the uniqueness of the setting because I was so on edge.

'When it became time, I was hustled into the courtroom, where I had to walk down a glass-enclosed passage inside the court – it's not a passage really, it's a seating area for the defendant. At the end of the glass-enclosed area, a door leads to the back of the courtroom and an internal stairwell. A female security guard ushered me through to the back, where I was meant to wait until the judge entered the courtroom and sat down. The guard patted me down to make sure that I wasn't carrying anything – a weapon or whatever.

'It was a peculiar place to wait, because it was simply a stairwell presumably leading to other parts of the building. It had just the one chair, where I was to sit and wait. I found myself wondering what they do with violent defendants in such a situation, and supposed that they are handcuffed or restrained in some manner. It all seemed surreal, like a scene from an old black-and-white film.

'The security guard kept poking her head around the door and looking into the courtroom to see whether the judge had arrived. From what I could see, the room appeared to be quite full. She came back to me saying that she'd never seen so many journalists in a courtroom before. She told me the crowd probably was there because a Category A defendant would be coming up. I asked what a Category A was, and she answered, "Someone who is a murderer." I looked at her and thought, well, it's possible, but I didn't believe that was the case this morning.

'"I think they might be here for me," I said. She seemed surprised and asked, "Why? What have you done?" I explained that I had leaked a memo about the Iraq War in an effort to stop it, and that I believed they were going to drop the charges against me. And it was a wonderful moment, because she patted me on the shoulder and said, "You go girl." It really made my day.

'The judge entered, took his seat, and the guard turned to me and said, "Right, you can go in now." I walked into a glass-panelled area, where I sat down, with everyone looking at me. I could hear all that was being said outside my glass box, but I felt completely alone. It was so different from the previous magistrates' court, where you sit next to your legal team. There, they call your name and you stand up to a podium of sorts. When the hearing is over, you return to sit with your solicitor. But here you are completely cut off from everybody else, completely alone in a glass cubicle. Isolated.

'The charges against me were read. I pleaded not guilty, and then the prosecutor, Mr Ellison, told the court the case would not go ahead for evidentiary reasons. Absolute silence. The charges truly were dropped! That quickly, that simply, after all that had happened since my arrest!

'Mr Ellison declined to explain the Crown's decision to discontinue the case. Ben Emmerson objected to the prosecution's refusal to offer an explanation. Further, he told the judge, there needed to be an investigation as to the who and why of the decision having been leaked to the *Guardian* six days before it was given to my defence team. He steamed a bit about the fact that eight months had elapsed since my arrest and the decision to charge me, and three more months since then.

'"Katharine Gun is entitled to know – and more importantly, the public are entitled to know," he said. Mr Ellison, of course, would not give any answers. He said that "consideration had been given" to what the Crown could appropriately say. Giving us reasons for their decision apparently was not considered appropriate.

'I looked around and everybody was standing up and getting ready to leave. As I walked out the other end of the glass cubicle, people started rushing toward me, mainly journalists, but also friends as well as onlookers I didn't know. James was immediately at my side and tried to protect me, but people kept reaching for me and saying, "Congratulations," and "Well done." To go from having felt so terribly alone a few minutes ago to being in the midst of so much attention was quite an emotional leap.

'We walked out of the courtroom followed by a crush of people, some shoving microphones at me, asking questions, asking for comments. James told them there would be a press conference at Liberty in the afternoon; there would be no interviews until then. Most moved back, apart from a lady from the BBC. She came hurrying up to us asking if I would give a live radio interview for BBC Radio 4's *World at One* programme. She was very persuasive, and I said yes.

'James and I were hustled down to the ground floor and into a back corridor, where a little room was set up for broadcasting. I put on headphones, and in this completely numb state of mind, I gave my first interview. It went out on BBC World Service as well. Around the world!

'Outside, there were dozens of photographers and journalists with their microphones and cameras waiting for us, calling to me. We decided it was best to speak with them briefly. As I walked over, a lady came up and handed me a bouquet of flowers. It happened so quickly that I didn't have time to catch her name or where she was from. And then I walked into the crowd of reporters and began answering questions.

'In the meantime, all of this was live on the streaming news channels, BBC News 24, and so on. Yasar hadn't come to London with me precisely because we didn't want any press attention on him. Given his tenuous residency status, it was best to keep him out of the picture as much as possible. He sat at home glued to the telly, watching me speaking live into the news cameras. At one point he saw me blinking back tears, and he began to cry.

'We escaped to a cab and went back to Liberty. I went for a walk, trying to get my thoughts together before the press conference. The reality of my freedom was just beginning to register.

'Liberty's offices were hardly suitable for a gathering like the one that followed. People were crammed into every nook and corner. It was a madhouse. The phones were ringing off the hook. Barry Hugill was taking phone calls from Reuters and journalists all over the world – he probably gave more interviews than I did that day. It was really an electrifying kind of environment. It went on forever, until my voice was hoarse.

'There was a brief break, and I sneaked into a small room to have a sandwich. A reporter followed me and continued to interview me while I ate. I could not fathom the attention, but then thought, "Of course, all of this is not really about me. It's about the war."

'At one point, when the lawyers were talking, I went upstairs and phoned Yasar on my mobile. With his voice breaking, he said that he'd been watching me on the telly, and then he started to cry, and I started to cry. And I just stood there, upstairs in the corridor of Liberty, crying my heart out. When we both calmed down, we talked about the fact that I had more interviews to do, but we agreed to meet afterwards. I suggested that he come up to London and that we go down to Brighton together. I said I would call him later to set a time and place to meet.

'My barrister came upstairs and found me. He could see that I'd been crying and gave me a huge bear hug. I felt a sudden, enormous relief. I finally allowed myself to feel all the emotions pent up for so long. I dried my face and went back downstairs to meet the journalists, including Jeremy Paxman, who has such a reputation for bullying.[6] Paxman was last, at the end of the day. The interview wasn't live, but we did it only once. At the end of it he said, "That wasn't so bad, was it?" And I said, "You said you'd be gentle on me, and you weren't!" He just chuckled.

'Later, I called Yasar, now in London, and arranged where we would meet. I picked up the bags I had packed for the next few days and flagged down a cab. My husband, my beautiful Yasar, was waiting for me in our little car parked on a street a distance away, just as we had planned. I jumped in beside him and we held each other and wept. It was over.'

It may have been over for Katharine Gun when the judge, the Recorder of London Michael Hyam, registered a formal verdict of not guilty, but it was far from over for Blair's government. Sir Menzies Campbell's prediction that dropping the charges against Katharine Gun would avoid embarrassment for the prime minister was dead wrong. What was to follow within twenty-four hours saw Blair red-faced and furious, one of his former cabinet members revealing devastating new UN spying secrets, heightened interest in Goldsmith's advice, demands for a retooling of the Official Secrets Act, and far too many people around the world cheering for Katharine Gun, who was the cause of much of his discomfort. Not helping was a statement the unrepentant former intelligence officer made to reporters outside the courthouse:

'I have no regrets. I would do it again.'

Whether her words came from a patriot or a traitor depended upon who was listening. We can safely surmise which description the beleaguered prime minister would have chosen.

CHAPTER 15: Reaction, Rebellion, and a Crushing New Revelation

I think people in GCHQ will know very, very well what is expected of them, and the Attorney General indicated very clearly it was on the particular facts of this case that the prosecution was dropped. But nobody should be in any doubt that we will apply the full rigour of the law to the greatest extent that we can do so, should people choose to breach the official secrets of the country.[1]

> – Tony Blair, on the collapse of the case against Katharine Gun

THE REASON FOR the prosecution's change of legal heart in the Gun case was the hot topic of the day immediately following the fall of Judge Hyam's gavel. Prosecutor Mark Ellison's statement, 'The prosecution offer no evidence against the defendant on this indictment, as there is no longer sufficient evidence for a realistic prospect of conviction,' made little sense. The facts of the case seemed to indicate that the prosecution had all the evidence it needed. Adding to a widely sceptical reaction was Ellison's announcement, 'It would not be appropriate to go into the reasons for this decision.'

For the Liberty team and most everyone following the case, going into the reasons seemed unquestionably appropriate.

Among the possible explanations for a government change of heart rehashed that day was GCHQ concern over additional unwelcome publicity about an employee who acted out of conscience. It would be best by far if GCHQ could melt back into its secret world and conduct its business without public commentary about consciences. Further, focus on the Gun case brought attention to the cosy GCHQ–NSA relationship. Katharine's statement made when she was charged only exacerbated the problem for the prosecution:

'Any disclosures . . . were justified . . . because they exposed serious illegality and wrongdoing on the part of the US government, who attempted to subvert our own security services.' Subvert our own security services! This was totally unacceptable to the British chauvinistic psyche. Further, Katharine's claim that she tried to 'prevent wide-scale death and casualties among ordinary Iraqi people and UK forces in the course of an illegal war' was a justification that resonated from coast to coast. It needled the UK public's strong anti-war feelings. Seating twelve unbiased British jurors could be a difficult prospect. With the strengthening winds of peace blowing across England, an acquittal could be likely.

But for most observers, the straw that broke the prosecution's already weakened resolve appeared to be the defence demand for evidence that the war against Iraq was, in absolute fact, legal according to the attorney general – a demand that would not, or could not, be met. On the Monday before, Harriet Harman, Goldsmith's solicitor general, made it abundantly clear that the government had no intention of publishing the attorney general's advice. As the prosecution folded, an unnamed government spokesperson insisted that the decision to drop the case was taken before the last-minute demand by the defence for documents, but few believed that this was the case.

'Katharine's counsel in court tried to press the prosecutor

to give reasons for the prosecution being dropped. As far as we can see, nothing substantial has changed in the last year since she was first arrested for this matter,' Liberty solicitor James Welch said. But of course something had changed. 'Late yesterday morning,' Welch said, 'we served on the Crown Prosecution Service a document in which we set out the rudiments of Katharine's defence, and made it clear what type of documents we'd be seeking.'

Welch did not say what so many were suspecting by now, that this last-minute request forced a last-minute decision. 'Whether that is what led them to drop the case or not, we can only guess,' a cautious Welch told the press.

Welch also raised another significant issue the government was hoping to avoid by ending the Gun case – pressure to revamp the Official Secrets Act. 'What this case shows,' he said, 'is that the Official Secrets Act must be urgently and radically reformed. People like Katharine, who highlight serious wrong-doing on the part of the security services, must not face prosecution and the prospect of prison.'

Like the young David who faced down a monumental Goliath, other members of the Liberty defence team made observations this day.

Director Shami Chakrabarti said the decision to charge Katharine had been 'political in the first place', adding, 'One wonders whether disclosure [of the requested documents] in this criminal trial might have been a little too embarrassing.' And Barry Hugill asked, 'Why have they waited until today? Why has she been put through eight months of hell?'

Press coverage of the dismissal of charges against Katharine Gun was phenomenal. Without the splash given elsewhere, even major US newspapers at least covered the story – the *Washington Post* and the *New York Times* among them. This, much to the amusement of *Observer* editor Martin Bright, who, with colleagues, had broken the original NSA story on 2 March the year before, when the US media had turned a blind eye to the bizarre spy case.

Interviewed by Alison Caldwell for Australia's ABC, Bright talked about the unusual end of the story.

'We are told that [the case] was dropped because there was insufficient evidence to proceed. It strikes me as rather absurd, considering Katharine Gun had admitted to the leak, which would seem to me to be the only evidence they needed.' Bright concluded that the issue was not evidence, but the government facing 'extreme embarrassment' over the Gun case, particularly with regard to legal advice on the war.

Foreign Affairs spokesman Sir Menzies Campbell put the end of the case simply and succinctly: 'This is a government retreat.'

One of the more widely quoted observations this day came from former spy Shayler, who said that a blanket of secrecy was used to protect intelligence matters that did not affect national security. And, 'If the intelligence services are going to do things that are illegal, they have to expect people to whistle-blow.'

The Crown Prosecution Service issued a formal statement immediately following the collapse of its case.[2] The reason for dismissal of charges was 'that there was no longer a realistic prospect of convicting Katharine Gun', Despite a 'clear prima facie breach' of the OSA as charged, 'The evidential deficiency related to the prosecution's inability, within the current statutory framework, to disprove the defence of necessity to be raised on the particular facts of this case.' Martin Bright's question comes to mind. She confessed, the evidence was concrete-solid, so what was lacking?

Most interesting in the document of explanation, which went on to describe the required evidential tests involved, is the following:

'This determination by the prosecution had nothing to do with any advice given by the attorney general to the government in connection with the legality of the war. It was also a determination made by the prosecution in advance of the defence request for disclosure, which came on 24 February

2004.' Further, it was made clear that the decision was made 'free from any political interference'. The very fact that these comments prefaced an explanation of evidentiary requirements only raised new questions. Among them, why, if the decision had been made to drop the charges days prior to the defence request on 24 February, had Liberty not been officially notified? Had it been, there would have been no need to continue preparation of its case.

If matters were uncomfortable for the government on the night of 25 February, they were about to become decidedly worse in very short order. The cause of much of the new setback, meanwhile, was enjoying a stay in Brighton with her husband and family.

On the morning of 26 February, it was reported that Lord Falconer, the constitutional affairs secretary, and Tessa Jowell, culture secretary, two 'loyal Blairites', were seen leaving the Westminster branch of Starbucks coffee shop looking as if the sky had fallen. Those who had listened to British national broadcasting over their own coffees an hour earlier were in a position to understand why the two prominent officials looked so terribly distressed.

The sky had indeed fallen, and all because MP Clare Short had been asked for her reaction to the Gun case. And, like the bombshell, it fell squarely on Tony Blair, which everyone noticed, and on George Bush, which only a few on his side of the Atlantic noticed.

MP Clare Short, interviewed on BBC Radio 4's *Today* programme, responded candidly to questions about the collapse of the government's case against Katharine Gun.

'This centres on the attorney general's advice that war was legal under Resolution 1441,' Short said. The advice was made public, she explained, but seemed to her to be 'very, very odd',

'My own suspicion is that the attorney general has stopped this prosecution because part of Mrs Gun's defence was to question the legality [of the war]. And that would have brought his advice into the public domain again, and there was something fishy about the way in which he said war was legal.'[3]

Short added, 'The tragedy is that Iraq is a disastrous mess. Ten thousand Iraqis have died, American troops are dying, some of our troops have died, and the Middle East is more angry than ever.' Not wanting to leave doubts about her position, she made it known that she saw government deceit in the run-up to war.[4]

These words were not the cause of the new uproar over the failed Gun case. Short was asked about the UN spy operation Katharine had revealed. Did the former cabinet minister think that sort of thing really went on within the United Nations? Perhaps even with someone like Secretary General Kofi Annan?

'Yes, absolutely. I read some of the [secret] transcriptions of the accounts of his conversations.' Here was direct, if unofficial, evidence that the secret service had been spying on the secretary general of the United Nations, clearly a serious breach of international law. 'Indeed,' Short continued, 'I have had conversations with Kofi in the run-up to war thinking, "Oh dear, there will be a transcript of this and people will see what he and I are saying."'

Clare Short had just leaked secret intelligence information! In the process, the colourful, controversial member of Parliament had committed a serious crime, boldly and publicly. She violated the Official Secrets Act, just as Katharine Gun had done. She could go to prison, if anyone dared to prosecute her.

More than a few people hearing this admission assumed that surveillance of Kofi Annan was a part of the same operation conducted by the United States, the United Kingdom, and their surveillance network – the operation exposed by Gun. It was a reasonable assumption. US and UK intelligence agencies work as a single entity at times, even to the point of sharing staff. Katharine Gun, for example, has had personal experience on US secret soil, the nature of which she will not reveal.

International media jumped on the Short revelation. 'UN rocked by allegations from former British Minister' was typical of the headlines written that day. Russia's UN ambassador, Sergey Lavrov, was interviewed by journalists and told them that, 'All this needs to be investigated by UN security.' In a lighter vein, Lavrov said he assumed 'this shows that the British intelligence services at least are very professional . . . but it's illegal'.

Annan's reactions were predictable. The secretary general would be disappointed if Short's allegations were true. Those who speak to him should be able to assume that their exchanges are confidential. An investigation would take place. If they exist, practices like those alleged must be stopped immediately.

By afternoon Fred Eckhard, Annan's UN spokesman, faced reporters. The first question asked was whether the 'practice of bugging the secretary general is regarded as illegal'.

Indeed, said Eckhard.[5] He cited three pieces of relevant international law: the 1946 convention on the privileges and immunities of the United Nations, which lays out the rules concerning the inviolable nature of its premises; the 1947 agreement between the United Nations and the United States, which places certain obligations on the United States with regard to the United Nations; and the 1967 Vienna Convention on Diplomatic Relations.

The exposed NSA operation had already violated all three. Eckhard's discussion of the laws brought attention back to the earlier revelations and to the woman responsible for them.

Short's disclosure could not have come from a higher level. It could not have been more devastating. Short had no doubt that the Koza invitation had been accepted, and she had personal knowledge that even Kofi Annan was not safe from this sort of skulduggery.

Later that morning, Tony Blair was deluged by reporters' questions about both Gun and Short. Transcripts of his press conference suggest a charged atmosphere and an uncomfortable session.

Beginning with Gun, the prime minister made clear that he 'played no part in the discontinuance of the prosecution'. The deciding factor was a 'belief that the prosecution could not secure a conviction based on legal and technical reasons'. When someone pointed out that substantial damage could have come from the defence demand for proof of the war's legality, Blair persisted in saying that he had no involvement in the case. But wasn't the attorney general a political appointee? Wouldn't that appointee want to please Mr Blair?

Nonsense, was the implication.

'If there had been some great political reason for not mounting this case it would have presumably been taken at the very beginning, not half way through it,' Blair said. This issue, of course, was not the mounting but the dropping of the case. The prime minister told reporters that he had spoken earlier in the morning with the foreign secretary, under whose direction GCHQ operates. 'The foreign secretary did not, like I didn't, play any role in the discontinuance of the prosecution.' It was for evidentiary reasons that the case ended the way it did, in spite, he said, of 'conspiracy theories that roll around'.

There was speculation in certain circles that a conspiracy of sorts did exist, that, unlikely as it seems, political pressure had been put on the Crown Prosecution Service to drop the case, independence and transparency aside. The thinking being that if this were the case, pressure exerted would have come from the director of prosecutions, who reports to the politically appointed attorney general. It is obvious that the attorney general was intent on serving the interests of Prime Minister Blair. Whether director of prosecutions Ken Macdonald leaned on prosecutors in some discreet way is a matter of almost delicious – and perhaps reckless – speculation for the conspiracy theorists.

Questioned about bugging Kofi Annan, the prime minister insisted that his government 'acted in accordance with domestic and international law'.

Blair was quickly challenged. Everyone, including Blair, agreed that spying on the secretary general was against international accords. Now, it was known that the United Kingdom (and almost certainly the United States) did precisely that, and yet the prime minister continued to insist that the secret service always acts only in accordance with the law.[6] There was a serious problem here. The press demanded answers. But the prime minister's response was to accuse the press of 'playing a game' with him, a game he refused to join. They were trying to trap him, and he wasn't about to be trapped. 'I'm not going to comment on the operations of our security services.'

Asked if he would support a prosecution of Clare Short for violation of the Official Secrets Act, Blair stumbled somewhat in his response. 'Well, as you know I don't – indeed, when we get on to discussing the other thing that happened yesterday [collapse of the Gun case], I don't deal with who is prosecuted and who is not prosecuted . . . I will say, however, that I really do regard what Clare Short has said this morning as totally irresponsible.' Blair's comment that the government would 'apply the full rigour of the law' against people who chose to breach the country's official secrets seemed to fall flat in the wake of Gun's escaping punishment and the likelihood that Short would do the same.

Asked if he considered it irresponsible to expose something his secret services were doing that was 'improper, something underhanded that the public would disapprove of', Blair responded that the services 'understand the legal framework within which they have to exist'. These pesky reporters were playing the game again, and Blair was getting huffy.

The prime minister commended Short for her work as development secretary, noting that there were many countries around the world grateful to her. But, 'It is a pity she has done what she has done today, because I think it is wrong.'

'After the collapse of the Katharine Gun case yesterday, isn't GCHQ going to leak like a sieve in the future?' someone asked.

Certainly not. The rest of the secret services staff was not like Gun. There would be no more leaks.

The issue of the war's legality as essential to Katharine's defence kept resurfacing. Blair continued to claim that there should have been no question. The war was in compliance with international law. The attorney general's opinion was clear and unequivocal. The killer question was one of the last: 'But did his advice change?' Essentially, did it change from questionable to unequivocal?

'No, I am sorry, the opposite is true. He counselled specifically that the war was lawful, otherwise we would not have gone to war. So it is absolutely clear what his advice is.' Here, recorded in the transcript of this day's press briefing, was the ultimate deception and the heart of the case against Katharine Gun.

The Sir Walter Scott rhyme ('Oh what a tangled web we weave') comes to mind.

Within two days, 25 and 26 February, Prime Minister Blair's comfort zone had shrunk substantially. His government failed in trying to put a confessed lawbreaker behind bars. He deplored the action of another lawbreaker, a former cabinet minister, but did not dare to have her prosecuted. His secret service was once again decried for unlawful and embarrassing spying on the United Nations. Difficult questions about the Iraq War's legality had shoved him into a corner that lacked space for honesty. A very bad two days, indeed.

It was not over for the prime minister. On 27 February, the *Telegraph*, noting Short's disclosure, reported reliable source allegations that UN chief weapons inspector Hans Blix had his mobile phone tapped during his time in Iraq, with details of his recorded conversations shared with Britain and the United States. No mention was made of who did the tapping. It is safe to say that few doubted the claim, and few wondered who was listening to the head of the team searching for Iraqi weapons of mass destruction.[7]

In Brighton, Katharine Gun, at least partly responsible for Blair's misery, felt no guilt. She was at peace with her conscience.

Across the Atlantic, the news that Katharine Gun would go free, the end of the story, had people wondering why they hadn't heard about the NSA spy operation at the beginning.

Perhaps, they reasoned, it was of little import in a grand scale of events dominated by focus on the war – the war President Bush had assured them was just and honourable and the essential battle in a fight against terror.

Now, a year later, George W. Bush was focusing on a different conflict – what some called 'the culture war'. Watching the international brouhaha from a safe distance, he had nothing to say about a renewed hostility toward the United States and its illegal spy operation. But he had a great deal to say about domestic issues, particularly gay marriage. Insisting he was 'protecting the institution of marriage', he stated his opposition to legalizing homosexual unions. A constitutional amendment might be the answer because 'the preservation of marriage rises to this level of national importance'. Another issue of national importance at the moment was pending gun control legislation, with the White House busy opposing the addition of gun show and assault weapons restrictions to a bill shielding firearms makers and dealers from lawsuits.

The fuming and fussing abroad about an NSA spy fiasco clearly were not a matter of national importance at 1600 Pennsylvania Avenue.

Fourteen months after the prime minister's assurance that day of a single, consistent opinion on the war's legality, the truth was leaked. Information made public by an anonymous source at Whitehall showed that Blair's response to questions about the attorney general's opinion had included at best a clever deception and at worst a deliberate lie.

This new and damning leak revealed that, as Wilmshurst claimed, Lord Goldsmith indeed had changed his opinion about the legality of a pre-emptive strike against Iraq. On 7 March 2003, the attorney general had given Tony Blair a thirteen-page opinion thoroughly supported by Foreign Office international law expertise, an opinion that expressed specific cautions about going to war under the existing sanctions. Ten days later, on 17 March, Lord Goldsmith, in an about-face, had presented a brief, written opinion to Parliament in which all doubt had been eliminated. There was no need for a new UN resolution; the contemplated strike against Iraq would be lawful under Resolution 1441. The first opinion was kept secret; the second, the go-ahead sought by Blair, was made public.

In his initial opinion, Goldsmith reviewed the three legally acceptable bases for the use of military force against another nation – self-defence, an overwhelming humanitarian catastrophe, and authorization by the United Nations. Meticulously, the attorney general examined all three, noting a lack of clarity, controversy, and ambiguity with regard to the issue at hand – whether the contemplated military action would be in compliance with international law without a new resolution.

Discussions and arguments Goldsmith presented were exhaustive. Previous resolutions were dissected with a sharpened legal scalpel. Also examined was the controversial issue of whether a threatened veto against a resolution for war could affect its legality.

More worrisome may well have been the cautions Goldsmith raised about the possibility of prosecution of the United States and the United Kingdom for crimes of aggression. However unlikely, it would be possible for opponents of military action to bring a legal case against both countries. But, Goldsmith warned, 'given the strength of opposition to military action against Iraq, it would not be surprising if some attempts were made to get a case of some sort off the ground'. And '*We cannot be certain that they would not succeed*' [emphasis added]. Under existing international accords, the United States and Great Britain *could* be charged with war crimes if they invaded Iraq without a lawfully sanctioned basis.

Finally, wrote Goldsmith, most significantly, '*Regime change cannot be the objective of military action*' [emphasis added].[8]

How ironic that regime change had been the objective of military action pushed by George Bush and agreed to (with stipulations later abandoned) by Tony Blair almost a year earlier, as reported in the 21 July 2002 Cabinet Office briefing paper.

Ironic as well that the Downing Street memo, dated two

days later, records Lord Goldsmith's discussion of the three acceptable reasons for an attack against Iraq, spelled out in a meeting with the prime minister and other senior UK advisers. He is reported as warning that 'the desire for regime change was not a legal basis for military action' – the phrase in his opinion given to the prime minister nine months later and kept hidden until it was finally leaked to the public.

The leak of excerpts from the attorney general's original opinion put enormous pressure on Blair to release its full text. Robin Cook, the former foreign secretary and leader of the House, who left Blair's cabinet over the pre-emptive strike on Iraq, had predicted this embarrassment. 'I urged the government to publish the full attorney general's advice, and warned that . . . it was inevitable that it would come out.'[9]

Inevitability struck at an especially inopportune time for Tony Blair. The leak surfaced just eleven days before the Labour Party and the opposing Tories were heading for poll booths. Blair survived, but with his power and party weakened.

Goldsmith's original position about the war was unambiguous and direct: 'The safest legal course would be to secure the adoption of a further resolution to authorise the use of force.'

The legality of the war was not only the defining issue in the Gun case, but also the defining issue in the history of one of the most controversial military conflicts in modern history.

In telling reporters following the collapse of Katharine's case that the attorney general's advice had never changed from his counselling 'specifically that the war was lawful', Tony Blair made a huge tactical error. And he was caught in a web of his own spinning.

CHAPTER 16: An Uncommon Day in the House of Commons

While we are left in this mystified state, it is fair for members to speculate about the reasons why this [Katharine Gun] prosecution was withdrawn. I wonder whether . . . there was a fear that no jury in the land would actually find this woman guilty . . . I wonder whether the substantive issue is being buried under the various legalities. The substantive issue is whether or not we acted at the behest of the American Government.

– Rt Hon. Colin Challen MP, in the House of Commons,
26 February 2004, 1.12 p.m.

A 'MYSTIFIED STATE' SEEMS to be where most members of Parliament were the day following the collapse of the Crown's case against Katharine Gun. Solicitor General Ms Harriet Harman was attempting to explain the Crown's position, hoping to extinguish the fires of anger heating up the atmosphere surrounding a distressingly significant number of sceptical members. Ms Harman had her work cut out for her, particularly with Mr Grieve, who was most troublesome.

She began her appearance before the House by reviewing relevant rules spelled out in the code governing Crown prosecutions. She explained that in addition to the two basic rules for prosecution, sufficiency of evidence and the public interest test, a prosecution under the Official Secrets Act has a third requirement. The attorney general must agree that the prosecution should go forward. She reviewed the Shawcross exercise, through which the attorney general asks ministerial colleagues for their thoughts and concerns about the proposed prosecution before a decision is made to prosecute. The exercise had been completed. All conditions had been met for Katharine Gun's prosecution. The Crown's case had been properly and meticulously prepared. Unfortunately, the case collapsed because of evidentiary issues.

As for the irritating nonsense that Attorney General Goldsmith's opinion on the war's legality played a role in the decision to drop the case – well, assured Ms Harman, that simply was not true. Absolutely, assuredly not true. It would soon become clear that her audience was not about to accept her absolute assurance.

What followed the solicitor general's opening remarks was amazing, even for the ever-rambunctious House. Attentive, focused, and to the point, members vigorously explored the basic issues of the entire Gun case, from start to finish. They asked all of the right questions, reflecting not only what their constituencies, but also many others around the world, wanted to know.

Following her lengthy opening statement, the solicitor general invited questions from her fidgety, explosive audience. First to respond was the honourable gentleman from Beaconsfield, Mr Dominic Grieve.

'This case raises some very important and worrying features. It is an unusual feature of the case, as the solicitor general will confirm, that the facts of Ms Gun's actions were not in dispute. The defence that had been raised was one of necessity . . .

'Was it the case that, prior to charge, the director of public prosecutions and the attorney general were consulted, so that the Shawcross exercise of which the solicitor general spoke was carried out? If so, why did the evaluation of the chances of conviction change so dramatically between the date of charge in November and the events yesterday? When did it become clear that the case would not succeed? When was it decided by the attorney general that it should not go ahead?'

Grieve continued with the observation that a decision to drop the prosecution was said to have been made prior to the 24 February defence request for information on the war's legality. Exactly when and why was this important decision made to drop the case? He noted that discussions had taken place between the attorney general and the foreign secretary on 14 and 24 February. Would the solicitor general kindly enlighten the House about those meetings?

In the event Rt Hon. Dominic Grieve had not been direct enough, he would be more specific:

'It has been widely suggested and publicized that the discontinuance followed a request by the defence for a copy of the attorney general's advice on the Iraq War. I cannot see a reason why the solicitor general cannot indicate whether such a request was made prior to discontinuance yesterday, and I would be grateful if she would tell the House whether that was indeed the case.'

She would, but not directly. The reason for ending the case had nothing to do with this persistent, ugly issue about the war's legality. It was because continuing reviews of the case prior to the date of trial revealed a problem.

'If at any point counsel decides, on balance of all the admissible evidence . . . that there is no longer a realistic prospect of conviction, it is counsel's duty to make his view known.' Discussions between the attorney general and foreign secretary on 14 and 24 February were only about evidentiary sufficiency. The obvious problem for some in the House was that nothing seemed to have changed between 14 November and the following 24 February regarding a sufficiency of evidence.

The honourable gentleman from Beaconsfield asked about

'new material' the government said had come to light, affecting the decision to discontinue the case. What, pray tell, was it?

Surely members must understand, Ms Harman had already explained, some secrets must remain secret. Although she would like to reveal more, she could not.

With regard to the evidence issue, the attorney general had said, and the solicitor general agreed, that the 'evidential deficiency' within the current statutory framework made it impossible to disprove Katharine's defence of necessity. This worried the member from Beaconsfield.

Grieve asked, 'Is the solicitor general saying that, under the Official Secrets Act, no defence of necessity can be rebutted? Or is she saying as Official Secrets Act prosecutions usually require the withholding of certain material from a jury under public interest immunity . . . that the current state of public distrust of the government over their actions in Iraq has rendered the process of justice impossible in this instance? Whichever is the case, this is a disastrous state of affairs for the due process of justice in this country.'

Mr Grieve said there had been previous requests by many people to see a copy of the attorney general's advice, which played so important a role in the Gun case. While there are acceptable reasons why this sort of request might not be honoured, would the government please consider waiving restrictions and allow the public to see that advice? Questions about this case and the whole war's legality issue could be settled. Would the solicitor general consult her cabinet colleagues about whether that might help restore faith in the administration of justice in this country?

'The honourable gentleman asked whether the government should waive confidentiality – whether either the prime minister or the attorney general should waive the normal rule, which is that legal advice to government is confidential. He suggested that it should be waived. I remind him that because of exceptional public interest in the question of the legal basis for the use of force in Iraq, the attorney general did, on 17 March, set out the basis on which he believed in the lawfulness of the use of force in Iraq; and he was able to reaffirm this morning, in another place, that his opinion of whether his view of the law was right had not changed.'

Later, of course, when the attorney general's original opinion of the war's legality was leaked to the public (and later released in full under pressure), it would become clear that Lord Goldsmith's opinion had indeed changed. Further, Elizabeth Wilmshurst's letter of resignation confirmed Goldsmith's switch to the approved 'official line'.

'No doubt many people will have examined the law on the use of force,' Ms Harman said, 'and, as we know from lectures and newspapers, many of them do not agree with the attorney general. If the attorney general tells the prime minister that he is entitled to do something, the prime minister is entitled to rely on that, irrespective of whether many other people take a different view.' She went further, saying the prime minister is 'obliged' to take the attorney general's advice.

Mr William Cash said, 'I hope that the solicitor general will understand when I say that I found much of what she said pretty unconvincing . . . With respect to the right honourable and learned lady's assertion that the prime minister is obliged to take his law from the attorney general, I refer her to a letter from the previous clerk of the house, Sir William McKay.'

Cash quotes from the letter: 'The law officers have no control over the legal action of the government. A minister is not obliged to take his law from the attorney general. Accountability thus rests with the ministerial decision-taker.'

Ms Harman insisted that the legality of an action was the business of the attorney general. She reiterated, 'The government have made it clear that they will not act in breach of international or domestic law, and they have only one authoritative source of legal advice, aside from the courts, and that is the attorney general.' Further, said the unhappy solicitor general, 'I am disappointed that the honourable gentleman found what I have said unconvincing because I have tried to be as clear as possible.'

Clear or not, the exchange did nothing to assure the House that the government had adhered to international law, as suggested by its refusal to rebut Katharine Gun's defence. Neither did the argument satisfy those who wanted the attorney general's opinion made public.

Amid the mutterings and outbursts typical of hot debate in the historic House, the member from Torridge and West Devon, Mr John Burnett, was recognized and raised questions about what had changed in the defence case between the time the defendant was first charged and the time the case was dropped. And then he moved on to a more threatening subject.

'Yesterday, counsel informed the court that the [Gun] prosecution was to be abandoned. The solicitor general will be aware that there has been considerable speculation that it was abandoned because the government feared that at the trial evidence would be adduced of the grave misgivings of many officials in a number of departments of state about the legality of the war with Iraq.'

Mr Burnett concluded with a charge that struck Ms Harman as most unkind, however respectfully framed: 'I respect both the attorney general and the solicitor general, but unless they put in the public domain . . . the compelling legal reasons for the withdrawal from the Gun prosecution, we can only assume that the law officers have capitulated to the executive, and have failed in their duty to the House and the country.'

She could not let that go. Capitulated to the executive? Failed in their duty to the House and the country?

'I take exception to the suggestion that the law officers have done that, and that the attorney general failed to carry out his duties as he was required to in this matter! Let me say most emphatically that he did not . . . The honourable gentleman said that many officials had misgivings. That might well have been the case, but the question of whether the prime minister had a lawful basis for the use of force is one on which he takes the advice of the attorney general. It is not for him then to second-guess that by taking the view of many officials who have misgivings.'

Unsatisfied, the honourable gentleman asked the terrible question that kept resurfacing. It was there, so prominently, because the case against Katharine Gun had collapsed in full view of the world.

Was there a connection between the discontinuance of the case and the request for disclosure?

Surely irritated by now, the solicitor general reaffirmed that 'the discontinuance was not connected to a request for disclosure of the attorney general's full legal advice or the anticipation of such a request being made'.

Her audience remained unconvinced.

Mr Denzil Davies of Llanelli spoke. 'Given the reasonable assumption that the defence of necessity must have been based upon a belief by the defence that the war was illegal, and since my right honourable and learned friend has said that the government would not be able to rebut that defence, does it not follow that the government are not able to disprove the assertion that the war was illegal?'

Of course it follows. But, replied Ms Harman, 'The defence of necessity can be based on many issues.'

Recalcitrant members returned to the issue of new evidence. Could whatever it was that torpedoed the Crown's case affect the potential success or failure of similar OSA cases? Sadly, she could not say.

Mr Donald Anderson of Swansea, East, asked about a great danger 'that other people in a position similar to that of Ms Gun will feel that they can disobey their obligations under the OSA and talk to newspapers'.

The solicitor general apologized to the House. Without her being able to share the intelligence involved, 'Members will not feel fully in the picture. But one of the characteristics of the security services is that people are supposed not to be put fully in the picture.' This must have come as something of a surprise to the members, who likely thought they should be in the picture.

Observed Mr Jon Owen Jones of Cardiff, 'Is not this case a very simple one, in that the government decided that they could not convince a British jury that they had gone to war legally?'

'That is not the case! My honourable friend is entitled to assert it, but I ask the honourable members at some point to believe what I have said.' Ms Harman acknowledged that her honourable friend might well be mystified by all of this.

Mr Jeremy Corbyn of Islington enquired as to whether it could be assumed that the government had accepted Katharine Gun's defence of necessity as overriding her loyalty to her employer, and that it would be reinstating her in the secret service.

'That is a very good question and I am actually going to answer it.' For a change, some surely thought. 'The government do not accept the public interest defence, of necessity.' Yet it dropped the case.

It was Katharine's good fortune that the honourable member from Cheltenham, Mr Nigel Jones, had been supportive throughout her ordeal. He had also been helpful in fighting her husband's deportation. His were the most personal remarks of the day.

'GCHQ is in my constituency, and Katharine Gun is one of my constituents. I have supported her through the recent difficult months, during which she has felt vulnerable, and I felt the relief that she experienced yesterday. Have the government given any thought to compensation for legal costs and any other compensation that it may be appropriate to give Ms Gun to help her rebuild her life?'

As if! thought many of the learned and honourable gathering. They were told that Katharine could apply for legal costs 'if so minded', and the processes would be applied in the usual way.

The questions did not become easier for the solicitor general; in fact, they became more dangerous. Mr Douglas Hogg, of Sleaford and North Hykeham, asked if she understood that 'many of us who opposed the war strongly suspect that in the government's possession are documents that . . . would have shown the war was unlawful and unnecessary'. Were there hidden documents that rendered the prosecution unable to rebut the defence?

Surely by now Ms Harman would cheerfully have strangled the honourable members who refused to accept her perfectly logical explanations about the law and the war and Katharine Gun.

'That is not the case,' she insisted.

Members next tackled the NSA spy operation and wanted to know if Ms Harman accepted that it was 'a clear violation not only of the Vienna convention on diplomatic relations, but – perhaps more importantly – of the 1946 general convention on the privileges and immunities of the United Nations'. Further, if the NSA–GCHQ operation had indeed taken place, 'those who authorised them and carried them out were themselves in breach of the law'.

Mr Michael Weir asked if an investigation would not be made into who was responsible for, and who had carried out, the spying scheme; further, he wanted to know, what action would be taken against the culprits. Clearly, the perpetrators resided at the National Security Agency, in Washington, DC, at GCHQ, and in London, although this was not said.

Ms Harman's honourable friend had placed her in an extremely difficult position. It is likely she knew her answer was a lie. As a senior law officer, she must have known the spy operation had in fact taken place, and she certainly was fully familiar with the international codes it had violated.

'All I can say in response to the honourable gentleman is that the government comply at all times with their international treaty obligations, as well as with domestic and international law.'

As the debate moved toward a painful and unsatisfying end, Mr Colin Challen of Morley and Rothwell agreed that the underlying issue, of going to war at the behest of the Americans, should be investigated and a report made to the House. The possibility of being dragged into an illegal war by the Americans was especially distasteful.

The answer to a final question, posed by Mr Hugh Robertson, dealt with organizational issues and not at all with the substance of his enquiry.

'Does the solicitor general accept that the government's inability to prosecute a civil servant who leaked state secrets to the press – particularly given that she worked at GCHQ – will send a shiver down the spine of every man and woman who works for our intelligence services?'

Who, Mr Robertson wondered, was going to protect the loyal people still working in the secret services?

'I should perhaps remind . . . that it is not the government who prosecute under the Official Secrets Act, it is the prosecution service.' As for protecting shivering spines, that was not a part of her territory. Someone else would have to deal with that.

Not quite thirty years old, Katharine Gun had shaken the House to its prominent and ancient foundations. Unfortunately, the colourful and compelling debate focusing on the legality of the war was not re-enacted in, and did not shake the foundations of, the Congress of the United States.

CHAPTER 17: Motivations, Misdeeds, and Tragic Mistakes

What was propelling the prime minister was a determination that he would be the closest ally to George Bush . . . his problem is that George Bush's motivation was regime change. It was not disarmament.

Tony Blair knew perfectly well what he was doing.[1]

— Former Cabinet Minister Robin Cook

Misdeeds may be due to passion, appetite, or ignorance.

— Plato

WHY DID THEY do it? Any of them? Katharine, Bush, Blair? Why did British cabinet officers feel compelled to resign in the weeks following Katharine's misdeed at Cheltenham? Were the white hats worn in the Gun saga truly white or simply politically bleached?

From the beginning of the Gun story, the most intriguing questions raised had to do with the Why of it all. Why would a young woman risk everything to do what she did? Why would two world leaders support such an embarrassing breach of international ethics? Who were the heroes, and who were the villains?

Motivating factors identified by Plato can be said to apply to heroics as well as misdeeds and, most appropriately, to the lead characters in the Gun story. Passion, on the parts of those wanting a war and those wanting to prevent or delay a war. Appetite, especially on the part of George Bush and company with their consuming hunger for taking out Saddam and their messianic, religion-driven fervour, for installing democracy in the Middle East. Ignorance, on the part of that same company, as well as on the part of Tony Blair for not predicting the inevitable chaos of an occupied Iraq and for failing to understand that their lies and deceit would ultimately be revealed. Ignorance on the part of Katharine Gun for believing she could remain anonymous and for believing her act of 3 February 2003 would not affect her life and that of her husband forever.

There is another 'why' issue: oil. For centuries the world has dealt with, or failed to deal with, tyrannical dictators who have robbed and murdered multitudes of their own people. But Saddam Hussein had oil. China was opposed to war with Iraq; China buys much of its oil from that country. The United States is a notorious oil glutton. It was clear to even the most gullible that oil had a role to play in the push to depose Saddam, regardless of denials to the contrary.

('It's the oil, stupid,' more than one pundit has said.)

The performances of the players in this true-life drama have been judged as heroics or as misdeeds, the rightness or wrongness seen in the eyes of the various audience members. Their actions, as well as those of certain other members of the cast, particularly Clare Short and law expert Elizabeth Wilmshurst, were considered bold and courageous by some and deliberate acts of betrayal by others. For many observers of the theatrics as they played out before an international audience, the defining issue was intent, born of correct or profoundly incorrect motivations. Not a bad platform from which to judge.

Contemplation of what motivates both courageous acts and misdeeds has intrigued the mind since the beginning of the human social experience. Such contemplation is both tantalizing and frustrating, for the answers to questions surrounding the performance of either are elusive and complex, more often speculative than certain. No one person can really know what is in the heart and mind of another. Even the best-trained professional can only judge by observation and listening. Personal truth, then, is subjective on the part of the observed and the observer. Still, with regard to this story, one is led to speculate, to draw certain conclusions about the truth, behaviour, and judgement of both.

No aspect of this sort of contemplation is more challenging than that concerning loyalty and its obverse, betrayal, as displayed for world view in this case.

Clearly, to some, Katharine Gun's behaviour was disloyal and bordered on treason. Inevitably, there would be heated controversy over exactly what motivated her action that morning in Cheltenham. She has been articulate in explaining her reasons, and some have believed her. Others have not. For some, a perceived 'Muslim connection' that inspired Katharine's lawbreaking has become like a chilling breeze that arises from time to time to disturb an otherwise rational piece of logic. There is no protection from this chill wind that continues to reappear. Those who believe in the existence of a secret commitment to Islam are not about to be convinced otherwise.

The reason offered by Katharine Gun for committing a serious crime and threatening her future is that she wanted to prevent an illegal war. It was a decision of conscience, simply stated and, perhaps, pitifully naïve. It is not good enough for many.

One of the most successful business leaders in the United States, former president and vice chairman of Chrysler and, at the time of this writing, chairman of General Motors North America, Robert Lutz was a Marine Corps attack pilot in the Korean War. The automotive guru is a keen observer of what makes people tick, certainly a key to his success. Lutz takes strong exception to Katharine Gun's violation of the Official Secrets Act, for whatever reason she offers.

'When you are under orders, you follow those orders, no matter what, no matter how you feel about what's happening,' he says. He considers her crime traitorous. Lutz piloted a plane carrying certain death, a payload he would release as instructed, whatever reservations he might have about just who would die as a result. Lutz sees only chaos resulting when a pilot or foot soldier or, indeed, an intelligence officer decides which orders and instructions he or she chooses to follow.

'She was wrong. It doesn't matter how she felt about the NSA operation, she was dead wrong,' Lutz says. 'When you have sworn allegiance, as Katharine surely did, you cannot simply "opt out" and decide that your moral judgement or misgivings justify betraying the system you voluntarily joined.'[2]

Similar feelings were expressed over a lunch in London, planned because of the nature of the two guests – keen and highly respected observers of not only the UK intelligence scene, but also of worldwide intelligence issues. Their opinions are sought, publicized, debated. The authors assumed the views of their guests would be the antithesis of their own, and thereby of special value. Their assumption was correct.

'I don't like her and I don't like what she did,' British intelligence consultant Glenmore Trenear-Harvey announced with typical Glenmore certainty. He was suspicious of Katharine's motives from the beginning. 'She'd been at GCHQ for two years. What did she think she was doing there?' And then, 'Did she plan this? Take the job and just wait to find something to leak?' Unconvinced by protests to the contrary, Glenmore repeated, 'I don't like her and I don't like what she did. She should have gone to prison.'

Across the table, prolific writer of intelligence books Nigel West agreed, at least insofar as Katharine Gun's leaking the infamous Koza e-mail. 'I have a problem,' the former member of Parliament said, 'with people who put themselves above their political masters, who pontificate, who think they know the truth – arrogant, like Katharine, they cannot possibly see the big picture.'

What one needs to understand, West said, is that intelligence officers work within their special microcosmic realms and have no knowledge of what is happening in the huge world of secrecy above and around them. To someone who is naïve or intent on deliberate harm, a specific piece of information collected might appear to be the proverbial smoking gun aimed at world peace. But it might be something else entirely. It might be, in whatever provocative colour and shape, simply a piece of a grand jigsaw puzzle belonging to the NSA's director or MI6's C. The point on which both luncheon guests agreed was this: An intelligence officer signs on for the duration and takes no action contrary to official instruction, adheres without question to the provisions of the Official Secrets Act, and remains loyal to the service under all circumstances. There is no excuse for, no reason for, doing anything else.

'She was a slight woman, blonde. Seemed naïve, innocent, well-meaning,' Glenmore said of Katharine. Emphasis was on 'seemed'. In the next breath, he mentioned a brief, recent chat with Jane Fonda. The actress's apology for her infamous mounting of a Vietcong anti-aircraft gun was intended to make her seem more naïve than guilty of a horrendous breach of patriotic ethic. But it didn't work. Fonda knew what she was doing and why; the reasons offered for her unseemly behaviour were clearly false – as were Katharine Gun's, insists Glenmore. Further, given the chance, Jane Fonda likely would not climb onto an enemy gun again, but Katharine would break the same law in a heartbeat. There can be no argument here; Katharine has said if she had it all to do over, she would leak the Koza message. A full-page colour photo of her appeared in the mainline British press with the statement, 'I would do it again' imposed in bold green letters below her right eye.[3]

There was no question that Glenmore and his various insider sources believed ulterior motives guided Katharine's hand on the morning of 3 February 2003. It was he who first suggested many months earlier that Katharine's motivation came via her husband, 'a Muslim', whose wife had converted to Islam, a religious connection she denies. Glenmore also reflected the Intel party line when he cautioned against meeting with Katharine. Stay away, he warned the authors. She is bad news.

'She swims in murky water,' Nigel said of Katharine, water teeming with 'protesters, ecological warriors, if not religious extremists'.

As for murky waters, the four of us meeting over lunch also swim in waters that are less than clear, sharing a shadowy ecology with present and former members of the intelligence community, with writers about intelligence, with the clubby bunch who train and teach and preach and sometimes reveal certain secrets of the deep. On this remarkably lovely early summer day, we divided straight down the middle with regard to Katharine Gun.

The timing of Katharine's action proved to be a serious problem for Nigel, who found it excusable that others have blown whistles for the sake of correcting, not making, history. Katharine leaked a vital secret when 'conflict was imminent. Her leak did not occur in a historical context, but at a time of peril,' he said, making her crime especially serious. Enter that pesky jigsaw puzzle again. It is acceptable to make a correction with regard to a specific piece or pieces, but only once the entire puzzle is completed by the knowing hand of the puzzle maker.

Nigel wanted the case against Katharine prosecuted and insisted that the reason for its collapse was not the need to keep under wraps Lord Goldsmith's original decision about the legality of the war, but simply that the prosecution did not believe it had a good enough chance of convincing a jury of Katharine's guilt.

'There has to be at least a 60 per cent certainty before the government will go ahead,' he said. He accepted the prime minister's statement that dropping the case was based on 'evidentiary and technical' considerations, not on politics.

The argument that the prosecution had eight months to figure its win potential and make the decision to charge and try Katharine carries little weight with those sharing Nigel's position. Neither does the argument that only one element changed after those eight months – Liberty's decision to challenge the government's insistence that the war had been found to be legal by the attorney general. Nothing else. Prior to that bold move, the percentage for prosecutorial success remained the same from March until November, when Katharine was charged and scheduled to appear in the Old Bailey; it was unchanged until the demand for information on Lord Goldsmith's opinion.

Looking at the principal players in the Gun drama, focusing on George Bush and Tony Blair, and considering the Platonic influences of passion, appetite, and ignorance guiding their great misadventure leads to some disturbing conclusions.

First, George Bush, 'leader of the free world'. There was his long-standing desire to 'take out' Saddam Hussein, one surely fuelled by Cheney's obsession and the hawkish inner circle surrounding him. Bush has been pictured as being cautious, reluctant to move toward war at times, but the Downing Street memos paint a different picture. Second, there was his naïve belief that his war against Iraq would be an easy in-and-out, essentially casualty-free exercise that would earn him the coveted historical distinction of 'war president'. This would ensure an enviable presidential legacy, unlike that of Jimmy Carter, who did not have the political savvy to get into a war. Third, and most frightening of all, given his White House occupancy, was that some suspect the president believed he was God's messenger destined to bring Democracy and Freedom, as he defined them, to the Middle East.

Looking at certain of the president's behaviours, noted clinical psychologist and author Dr Peter O. Whitmer finds intriguing possibilities in autistic logic, a mental certainty that can 'seduce, inspire, and propel leaders of nations and groups'. It is a force, says Whitmer, 'beyond the reasonable logic of reasonable men, energizing pursuit of extreme devotion, conviction and certitude'. It is a behaviour that differs markedly from the usual image of silent autistic withdrawal from reality and society.

Extremism is key and 'cuts both ways', according to Whitmer. 'There are extremes of both achievement and progress, bigotry, self-righteousness and downright pig-headedness.' In autism, he says, one finds 'the deepest well of human motivation, the most profound determinant of the "why" of one's behaviour. Autistic thinking,' concludes Whitmer, 'is zeal personified, a fuelled focus – a gift to some, destruction for others.'[4]

For the record, Bush's stated motivation can be found in numerous speeches and comments given to the press, to the public, and to Congress. Saddam Hussein had failed to comply with United Nations Security Council resolutions in the past, was continuing his obstructionist behaviour, had countless storehouses of weapons of mass destruction, and was an imminent threat not only to his neighbours but also to the entire world. It is likely Bush believed every word. He hardly mentioned regime change, prohibited by international law as the primary justification for attack, until the WMD rationale fell flat.

As for Tony Blair, it seems apparent that he was motivated by the critical need to maintain a mutually supportive, politically and historically unique relationship with the United States. Further, lawyer Blair, politically more astute than his colleague across the Atlantic, did not go along with a distasteful, worrisome policy because he liked Bush's famed barbecue served to foreign dignitaries visiting the president's Texas ranch; rather, he did so because he hoped to influence policies decided there. It can be argued that he was deeply concerned, from the very beginning, about a wild-eyed US administration, ill-prepared and without international support, prematurely launching a war against Iraq and dragging along a reluctant, also ill-prepared, British partner. He was willing, to this end, to suffer the humiliation of being depicted in British newspaper cartoons as a curly-haired poodle being led by a tiny cowboy in an oversized Stetson and cowboy boots.

A British civil servant, speaking anonymously, claims that it is widely believed in government circles that Mr Blair was anticipating the establishment of a 'United States of Europe'. Standing strongly for principles that would define this new union, and standing against Saddam Hussein and his threats to the rest of the world, could polish Blair's image as a leader. Blair could be seen as the obvious choice for the role of president of the new international body.

Blair explained a motivation – not the one noted above, but one for public consumption – as being consistent with that of George Bush. 'I have been increasingly alarmed by the evidence from inside Iraq that despite sanctions, despite the damage done to his capability in the past, despite the UN Security Council Resolutions expressly outlawing it, and despite his denials, Saddam Hussein is continuing to develop WMD, and with them the ability to inflict real damage upon the region, and the stability of the world.'[5]

In the end, when the WMD argument was found to be flawed, when there was increasing concern that the pre-emptive war had been illegal, when public outrage was beginning to swell, both Bush and Blair told the world that the war against Iraq was justified, weapons or no, because Saddam was a bad man. More than that, he was a monstrously bad man who had inflicted untold horror on segments of his own country. The argument was failing to grow sufficient legs, for more than one monstrous despot had murdered and was murdering segments of the population. The new motivation sounded disturbingly and primarily like regime change.

On occasion, the media have referred collectively to three women characters in the Gun drama: Katharine, Clare Short, and Elizabeth Wilmshurst. Together, they have been represented as being of a single mind about the war, with each taking a very public and determined stand. In the process, Short and Wilmshurst appear to have been kind to and supportive of Katharine; she is deeply grateful and has great respect for both women.

Clare Short's revelations about misdeeds in the British secret service were to Tony Blair, and even to some members of her own Labour Party, an act of betrayal; yet she has fans who admire and respect her gutsy stand. 'People may turn away from me in Parliament,' she says, 'but outside, on the street, they come up to me and thank me.' Short spoke out about spying on Kofi Annan because she believed what was happening was morally wrong and, finally, had to be acknowledged.

Political opponents find it easy to argue against Short, considering her an outspoken, flamboyant woman whose liberal-soggy brain is as sharp as a jar of crumbling British biscuits. To tattle on the British secret service was criminal, and some still insist she should have been prosecuted for violation of the Official Secrets Act. As for her resignation from Blair's cabinet, some still question her motivation; yet she has made it abundantly clear that her decision to leave was firm from the beginning. She left, although belatedly, because she believed the pre-emptive attack on Iraq was a violation of international law, which lays out the rules for war.

'The cause has to be just,' she says. 'Any use of force has to be proportionate. Most important, it must be the last resort.'

Short's explanation for her action makes sense. Iraq was a problem that could not be ignored; however, it was a problem that could be solved in a way far more constructive than going to war. She had solid, specific recommendations that at least deserved a fair try. But in the hurricane-force winds blowing toward war, her voice was lost. She took a stand to make a life-and-death point.

The motives of Clare Short and Katharine Gun have been challenged, but not those of Wilmshurst. It has been far too difficult a task to find an ulterior motive for the former Foreign Office deputy legal adviser who had nothing to gain and everything to lose by taking a risky public stand against her prime minister and attorney general.

Wilmshurst's motivation was made clear in her letter of resignation of 18 March 2003, which was censored, leaked, and released in full in 2005. An offending paragraph had been withheld, said the government, 'in the public interest'. Shadow Foreign Secretary Sir Menzies Campbell had a different view. 'The government didn't withhold it in the public interest, it withheld it in the government's interest.'

In her letter, Elizabeth Wilmshurst wrote, 'I regret that I cannot agree that it is lawful to use force against Iraq without a second Security Council resolution to revive the authorisation given in SCR 678. I do not need to set out my reasoning; you are aware of it.'

What follows is the key paragraph withheld by Blair and company:

'My views accord with the advice that has been given consistently in this Office before and after the adoption of UN Security Council Resolution 1441 and with what the attorney general gave us to understand was his view prior to his letter of 7 March.'

And then, in parentheses, what troubled the legal expert most of all: '(The view expressed in that letter has of course changed again into what is now the official line.)'

In confirming that Lord Goldsmith had, indeed, changed his opinion about the legality of going to war, Wilmshurst was confirming her own integrity. She would not go along with 'the official line', would not violate the moral ethic that had guided her professional life. Wilmshurst, throughout her career, was committed to compliance with the law and thus with clearly defined international codes binding both Britain and America.

Finally, it is helpful, especially for Americans, to consider the action of the late Robin Cook, the prestigious leader of the House of Commons, who resigned that post in the midst of heated debate over the Koza leak and the failure to secure a second UNSC resolution for war. Pre-emptive war, he knew, would be fully under way within days. Cook, intelligent, loyal, could not in clear conscience support a war without true international agreement and without domestic approval. And the absence of both was painfully obvious to the veteran British politician.

Cook's statement that history would be 'astonished at the diplomatic miscalculations that led so quickly to the disintegration of that powerful coalition' evidenced his deep concern for governance gone profoundly wrong. He was willing and determined to give up a brilliant career rather than be led by diplomatic miscalculations of such monumental significance.

During his four years as foreign secretary, from 1997 to 2001, Cook was in part responsible for the Western strategy of containment, a strategy that had crippled Saddam's ability to make war. 'Iraq's military strength is now less than half its size at the time of the last Gulf war,' he said as he resigned on 17 March 2003. This was hardly a regime in the position of threatening Britain and the United States or even its neighbours. Unable to convince Blair of this fact, Cook had to leave his post. It was the decent and honourable thing to do.

What may make Cook's comments upon resigning that day of particular interest to Americans is this observation, part of his farewell speech: 'What has come to trouble me most over past weeks is the suspicion that if the hanging chads in Florida had gone the other way and Al Gore had been elected, we would not now be about to commit British troops.'

In the end, the powerful leader of the House of Commons broke ranks with his prime minister – a necessity based on principle and conscience. Katharine Gun's defence was based on the concept of necessity. It was necessary for her to act according to her conscience, necessary to try to save British lives. An unanticipated outcome was that others in the intelligence/government community followed her lead, and a dam of secrecy crumbled as more and more deceit and outright lies were exposed to a dismayed public by 'leakers', whistle-blowers dealing with conscience and necessity.

Considering motivations, the heroes and the villains are not easy to identify in this drama. A worldwide and highly critical audience must sift through the evidence, examining the motives behind actions planned in laid-back Downing Street offices – where, it is said, a barefoot Tony Blair held meetings of import – and strategies discussed in Crawford, Texas, in the cab of a dusty pickup truck, with a blue-jeaned driver and a foreign head of state in the passenger seat.

CHAPTER 18: Whistle-Blowing: Conscience and Confrontation

What has to be understood is that most whistle-blowers are not natural activists – this one certainly wasn't. We usually work in anonymous jobs, far from the spotlight. We are not campaigners or journalists or wannabe celebrities craving a platform. Our conscience tells us we must reveal what we know. We do that, we blow the whistle, and overnight the whole media circus descends on us. You just don't know what to do . . . that's why we stick together.[1]

– Katharine Gun

SPEAK OUT, KATHARINE Gun invited government workers. Speak out when you have information about illegal government activity. Coinciding with the third anniversary of her arrest, published in the British press but directed to Americans as well, her invitation pointed to ominous similarities between Iran nuclear-threat rhetoric and the rhetoric that preceded the pre-emptive strike against Iraq. It all sounds too much like military inevitability. What are the facts, she wanted to know, and what, instead, is politically driven hype spun by the same sources who fictionalized the WMD story? Where does the truth lie, and who will tell it?

Katharine admits, 'The fact that Iran thinks its answer to generating power lies in nuclear energy is worrying.' But she finds the cause of worry not in the possibility of weaponization, which can be monitored, but rather in the critical problem of maintaining safety. 'We should be encouraging Iran to seek safer alternatives, just as our environmentalists lobby governments to seek safe, renewable sources of energy.'

In addressing government workers, Katharine said, 'follow me'.

One must ask – follow her where? To a promising career forever destroyed? To the possibility of years behind prison bars? To a life where earning a modest living is an unrelenting struggle, to where even decent, honourable people think she should have been executed? There are still some who feel this way, including the wife of a distinguished British diplomat who told the authors more than three years after the case against Katharine collapsed, 'They should shoot her.' This, from an intelligent, well-educated, thoughtful, and seemingly caring person.

Despite angry comments from her detractors, Katharine continues to urge those 'in a position to do so' to disclose misleading or false information from government sources. For example: 'Don't let intelligence be fixed around policy ever again.' Expose the prevaricators. And do it now, not later.

The issue of immediacy is one that whistle-blower icon Daniel Ellsberg stressed when praising Katharine Gun for revealing the NSA spy plot within days of learning of it. Ellsberg delayed in leaking the Pentagon Papers until 1971 – a mistake, he says, and one he sorely regrets. American lives could have been saved in Vietnam if only he had gone to the media a year earlier.

'Like so many others, I put personal loyalty to the president above all else – above loyalty to the Constitution and above obligation to the law, to truth, to Americans, and to humankind. I was wrong.'[2]

Ellsberg believes that Katharine's revelation was critical in denying the attack an acceptable legitimacy. To Ellsberg, Katharine is the ultimate model for whistle-blowers: conscience-driven with a keen sense of timing.

Katharine, much in the way Ellsberg does, talks about the crushing ramifications of egregious government deception, and what could have been – a war averted, lives saved, respect for international accords, confidence in the integrity of government.

In the centre of the spin, in the eye of the rhetorical vortex, was the Big Lie. 'It's been more than four years now, with the knowledge that there were no WMD in Iraq, that the intent was regime change all along, that because of the lie, lives were destroyed and hundreds of thousands have suffered untold misery.' Do we think, she asks, that those who set out to invade Iraq on false charges are 'too bogged down in Iraq and Afghanistan' to take similar action against Iran? Or, perhaps, somewhere else in the Middle East?

In December 2007, an unnamed individual (who may or may not have been aware of Katharine's appeal to potential whistle-blowers) revealed that her former agency, GCHQ, had been involved in espionage operations against Iran. Not only that, GCHQ had, of course, been sharing that intelligence with the United States. In Washington, 'speaking on the condition of anonymity', a source leaked the news that British intelligence gatherers were so occupied. No doubt, data collected were invaluable in developing the US National Intelligence Estimate on Iran's nuclear programme.[3]

It can be assumed that the wires continue to hum productively on Menwith Hill and at the NSA in Maryland. Togetherness in the world of the listeners.

Katharine was first approached to speak out against war shortly after the case against her collapsed and while she was still very much in the news. The invitation came from the UK Stop the War Coalition, an organization that frequently holds rallies in Central London locations like Trafalgar or Parliament Square, often drawing huge crowds. Katharine declined.

'At the time, the thought of speaking out in front of hundreds or even thousands of people scared me.' There was an even more important reason for declining. 'I also didn't want to draw additional attention to myself, as Yasar's immigration status had not yet been settled. Our main focus at that time was to try and find a solution to allow him to remain in the United Kingdom with me.'

Katharine's reluctance to make public appearances lessened as time went on, although being in the political limelight was not easy. It was not simply a matter of shyness. Katharine believed the secret service remained quite interested in what she did and said.

'I was terribly nervous when I talked about what had happened. My heart raced, my hands shook, and I felt as though I were reliving that frightening period of time. It's only in the last year or so that those feelings have subsided, only now that I'm more confident about speaking in public,' she said in late 2007. There has been no official negative reaction to her appearances thus far. But she does not delude herself. It could come at any time.

Anyone watching Katharine on television or listening to a radio interview would never suspect that she had ever felt insecure or frightened. She is articulate, poised, seemingly confident. There is no hesitancy, no struggle for words, as she discusses war and peace, global ethics, international accords. She is, as some have said, 'a great interview'.

'I was, and still am, torn about what I should now do, about what more I can do,' she admits. 'My close friend once said that many people try to speak out, but no one listens because that person has no platform. She said I have a platform and I should use it. But, looking back, it didn't come naturally to me, and I decided to be selective about what I said and when I said it.' There are times, she notes, when it is absolutely essential to take a stand.

Katharine says, 'Truth telling and whistle-blowing are crucial after a war as ill-advised as Iraq.' If the truth had been known by the public earlier, perhaps Saddam Hussein could have been disposed of through other means, potentially effective strategies ignored by two governments secretly set on war. The truth did indeed come late, long after that first leak of Katharine's, when others in government and the intelligence community followed her lead, including bold, outspoken Clare Short. Still, learning the truth even now allows 'piecing together the facts', a piecing together that, if the world is ready to learn, may well avoid further chaos and destabilization in the Middle East.

At every opportunity, Katharine continues to press for truth telling, both in the United States and abroad. Is she encouraging others to break the law? Yes, indeed, would answer the 'let's shoot her' proponents; absolutely not, would answer the whistle-blowers.

The potentially deadly international implication of manipulation and falsification of intelligence is only one reason for speaking out on both sides of the Atlantic. Without someone's telling the truth, Americans would not be aware of shocking dirty secrets that have so dishonoured their country since 9/11 – the clandestine 'terrorist flights' to foreign countries for the purpose of torture, the brutal and humiliating treatment of prisoners and detainees in US care abroad, the disgraceful and absolute disregard for the Geneva Conventions. British citizens would not have learned about Tony Blair's blatant deception concerning Lord Goldsmith's opinion on the war's legality, the real substance of the prime minister's pre-war meetings with George W. Bush, or the misleading and false statements in the infamous 2002 Iraq dossier. They would never have known of the attack on truth that, like a disease, plagued the days before the war.

It seems appropriate that the word whistle-blower originated in the country where Katharine was born, used in reference to uniformed bobbies whose whistles signalled discovery of a criminal act. Wherever used, the word conveys a very distinctive meaning clearly understood by everyone who has revealed secret information – trouble. Trouble for the person with the whistle and trouble for the reason it's blown. It means pain, sometimes agonizing and, almost always, of lengthy duration. To blow the whistle on a perceived wrong is an act of courage or foolishness or a bit of both. Not everyone gets caught, but everyone is fearful.

Those who reveal illegal or embarrassing government secrets pay, as Katharine did, a high price for their acts of conscience. Like her, they pay in the currency of lives interrupted and careers destroyed, of being called traitors at worst and unpatriotic at best. Whistle-blowers have to be tough and determined, knowing full well the measure of the opponents and the height of the deck stacked against them. There are wounds that do not heal, even when someone wins, as did prestigious social scientist Dr Marsha Coleman-Adebayo. Settlement of her case against the US Environmental Protection Agency included a $600,000 award from the government.[4] But win or lose, whistle-blowing is no game for sissies. All of which make some of the most improbable of this category the most courageous.

'There is something about Katharine Gun that makes her seem an unlikely candidate for whistle-blowing,' observed BBC political staffer Ben Davies.[5] And yet, Davies continues, 'this rather shy thirty-year-old' had leaked details of the NSA spy operation against members of the UN Security Council. Davies's first impression of Katharine was on target. Meeting her is an unsettling experience; she is hardly what one expects. There is a poignancy, a legitimacy, a sweetness about her that is inescapable. One expects toughness, an obvious fighting spirit, even a bold recklessness. Perhaps conscience, in her case, works quietly and doesn't neon-light itself in this petite, courteous young woman.

What is frankly astonishing is that so many other whistle-blowers also seem to be 'unlikely' candidates, high-level, distinguished government workers or seemingly unremarkable, 'ordinary' people. A diverse group of individuals sharing a common experience, they are a global ethic in human form. This coming together of the like-minded has resulted in initiatives to encourage and support whistle-blowers through the establishment of dozens of truth-telling alliances – like the informal group Katharine helped bring together – and organizing high-profile meetings, some focusing on government and some on the private sector.

In May 2007 forty public interest organizations participated in the Whistleblower Week in Washington, its purpose to highlight contributions of whistle-blowers and to garner congressional support for restoring and strengthening legislation protecting federal whistle-blowers.[6]

At one of the first events that week, author Marcia Mitchell was asked to testify on the Katharine Gun/NSA/GCHQ case and appeared before a distinguished Capitol Hill panel. Hers was the only testimony relating to involvement of a foreign government in a domestic operation. Katharine, whose job in England kept her from being present, was there in spirit. The part-time teacher of Chinese cannot afford to miss work.

The list of sponsors and organizers of the historic Whistleblower Week in Washington evidences a broad base of support. They include the National Whistleblower Centre, the National Treasury Employees Union, the No Fear Coalition, the American Federation of Government Employees, the American Civil Liberties Union, the Project on Government Oversight, the Government Accountability Project, Whistleblowers USA, Common Cause, the US Bill of Rights Foundation, the Union of Concerned Scientists, and a great many others. It was an amazing and diverse coalition.

There is no question that momentum for organizing has been building over the years since the Iraq War was launched. In September 2004 Katharine was invited to attend an American University symposium in Washington, DC, 'When Silence Is Complicity', the first-ever gathering of high-level national security whistle-blowers. Here Katharine spoke before a packed auditorium of faculty and students. And it was here that British Katharine and Americans Daniel Ellsberg and prestigious former CIA intelligence analyst Ray McGovern joined in the informal truth-telling alliance, here in the US capital that she met so many others like herself.

'This was the first time I'd met Sibel Edmonds, Coleen Rowley, and others who had spoken out before and after the war on Iraq,' Katharine says. 'I felt at home and part of a supportive network with these wonderful people.'

Edmonds was fired by the FBI and Rowley was allowed to retire from the Bureau after both leaked information concerning the 9/11 terrorist attacks. They are seen as heroes throughout the whistle-blower community. All three women – Gun, Edmonds, and Rowley – have been recognized by the Sam Adams Associates for Integrity in Intelligence, a group of mainly former CIA colleagues promoting truth telling.[7] The organ-ization honours devotion to truth, 'no matter the consequences'. The annual Sam Adams award went to Rowley in 2002, Gun in 2003, and Edmonds in 2004.

Also participating in the American University symposium was Maj. Frank Grevil, a Danish intelligence officer arrested for leaking pre-war classified documents reporting that no weapons of mass destruction would be found in Iraq. Parallels were drawn between Gun and Grevil. Both intelligence officers, just weeks before the war was launched, provided the media with critical secret information potent enough to raise public ire and create political upheaval.[8]

Katharine had met Grevil earlier, during an anti-war confer-ence in Denmark. It was her first public appearance of this nature, a hearing on the Iraq War convened at Christianborg, on 15 April 2004 – not quite two months after the case against her had collapsed.

'One reason for putting together our informal coalition was to help people like us, like Frank and Coleen and Sibel, hold their lives together when the going gets tough and, honestly, it does,' Katharine says. 'And Sibel, probably more than most, knows just how tough it can get.'

Edmonds lives with court decisions and media restrictions that are extraordinary – 'Kafkaesque', she says. Not only were all records associated with her case retroactively reclassified as secret, but also every government document bearing Edmonds's name or birth date – like her driver's licence and passport.

The government has been kinder and gentler with Rowley. Rowley claimed the agency bungled a chance to thwart the 9/11 attacks by blocking Minneapolis agents from searching the possessions of jailed terrorism suspect Zacarias Moussaoui. In Rowley's case, then FBI director Robert Mueller promised there would be no retaliation and granted her permission to publish articles about civil liberties, ethics, and integrity. Intelligence guru McGovern credits Rowley with a monumental achievement. 'If it weren't for Coleen Rowley, there would have been no 9/11 commission . . . The whole thing would have been covered up.'[9]

Coming at this time was the Truth-Telling Project, an effort to encourage whistle-blowing by government workers, a project Katharine applauded.

Daniel Ellsberg explained it this way: 'The project urges current and recently retired government officials to reveal the truth to Congress and the public about governmental wrong-doing, lies and cover-up. It aims to change the norms and practices that sustain the cult of secrecy and to de-legitimize silence that costs lives.'[10]

In a letter seeking 'Patriotic Whistleblowers', the project wrote, 'Thanks to our First Amendment, there is in America no broad Official Secrets Act [as in the more restrictive United Kingdom], nor even a statutory basis for the classification system' – which should be encouraging to those considering going public with insider information (but could hardly be reassuring to Sibel Edmonds).

There are only three types of information whose disclosure is expressly criminalized by the US Congress, explains the letter: communications intelligence, nuclear data, and the identity of US intelligence operatives. This last, of course, is what got Lewis 'Scooter' Libby into trouble. The first, had she been a US citizen, would have done the same for Gun.

The project called for specific documents that deserved

disclosure, including several concerning 'prisoners from the war on terrorism', reports on inquiries into intelligence activities before and after 9/11, redacted segments of various other government reports, and predictions and analyses focusing on the post-war occupation and restoration of civil government in Iraq.

Well understanding a reluctance to respond to its call, the project cautions that doing so can entail danger and the inevitable high cost. But a 'continued silence brings an even more terrible cost'.

It was a 'continued silence' that Katharine Gun's conscience rejected.

It would seem that fired senior intelligence analyst Mary McCarthy was the ideal respondent to whistle-blowing pleas from both Ellsberg and, later, Gun. McCarthy was sent packing in 2006 for leaking information to the media on the CIA's prisons abroad, precisely one of the disclosures called for in the project's appeal. It appears that McCarthy was one of the sources *Washington Post* reporter Dana Priest used in researching the secret prison story that won the journalist a Pulitzer as well as outrage about her lack of patriotism.

An 'unnamed former senior intelligence official' said most CIA officers would agree that McCarthy should be among the missing at the agency. After all, he said, 'the ethic of the business is not to leak'.[11]

McCarthy's detractors say she should have stayed within official channels rather than going to the media. 'This is what they've said about me,' Katharine says, noting the similarity between her leak and McCarthy's. 'But my complaint would have been lost in bureaucratic red tape. Nothing would have happened if I'd worked within the system.'

Katharine worries about the fate of whistle-blowers and leakers. She has said that, although she was arrested and charged with high crime, she paid far less for telling the truth than did UK weapons expert Dr David Kelly, whose death still troubles her. Kelly died following the Blair government's naming him as the source of information regarding 'sexing up' pre-war Iraq intelligence.

Controversy over Kelly's death – suicide or murder – led to an investigation chaired by British Law Lord Hutton. Hutton concluded that Kelly was a suicide, who 'probably killed himself because of extreme loss of self-esteem'. Chalk up one dead whistle-blower, killed by deception, vindicated long after the truth was leaked about sexing up WMD intelligence.

'I fared far better than he did,' Katharine says.

Because of Katharine Gun's criminal act two weeks prior to the strike against Iraq and the acts of those who followed her lead – sometimes, like Kelly, at great cost – a saddened public has learned about the insidious and clandestine use of deception and nuance as tools for political purpose. This has been particularly true when the purpose is to ratchet up fear and to gain support for controversial and perhaps illegal measures taken in the name of national security.

A fearful populace can be kept silent and acquiescent by the spectre of evil terrorists ready to strike the United States once again. This is not to say that the threat does not exist, but rather that, because of it, exaggerated fear and irrational response can be manipulated at will.

Just like in the Cold War, when the feared bogeyman was a Communist said to be lurking in every corner of government, in neighbours' homes, and on university campuses across the country.

CHAPTER 19: A Life Interrupted

Thanksgiving is just around the corner. I've been trying to find more work besides teaching, but without success. I'm trying to remain positive – poor hubby gets hurt when I'm miserable and worried, but it's very hard to see any improvement in our situation.

– Katharine Gun, 2007

KATHARINE'S LEGAL BATTLE ended on 25 February 2004, but not that of her husband. Deportation had threatened Yasar Gun twice. His visa had been extended more than once but would not be again. His request for political asylum was denied. Further, he would not be allowed to apply for residence while on United Kingdom soil, even as the husband of a citizen; instead, he would be deported.

One option existed – Yasar could leave the United Kingdom and apply for residency from another country. This would not immediately ensure permanent status but would be a step in the right direction. The problem: time was very much of the essence. Visions of Yasar being picked up by law officers and put on a plane were vivid. This time, the plane might leave with him on board, with no last-minute rescue as before.

The Guns decided that whatever they would do, they would do it together. If they travelled abroad to apply for Yasar's residency and he was denied re-entry, Katharine would remain with him and not return as well. But if they went abroad and were allowed to re-enter, all would be well. Otherwise, the United Kingdom would see the last of both of them.

One wonders if this prospect might have been extremely appealing in certain government circles.

Messages to the authors during this period revealed that Katharine and Yasar were desperately concerned about leaving the country with no guarantee of a return visa. But time was running out, and, with no other choice and with great trepidation, they hurriedly left home.

For a few days, there were no messages until, with great relief, Katharine wrote, 'All is well!' Legal requirements for Yasar's UK residency application had been met; it would be safe for him to return to England in a few days, his wife at his side. The couple, for the first time since the infamous NSA message was sent, felt what had been an emotionally crippling tension slip away, replaced – at least for a time – by a soaring, absolute joy. They had a carefree holiday, a honeymoon, a celebration. They even dared to hope for a 'happily ever after' ending to their story.

In many ways, it has eluded them.

Returning home, the Guns faced problems like those confronting most young couples, except that theirs were exacerbated by all that had happened since Katharine's arrest. The construct of a typical life had not been theirs, except for those few months before Katharine's arrest, when Yasar's work was less difficult and Katharine had a secure, well-paying job. Before the media discovered Katharine Gun.

Inevitably, as time went on, the debilitating pressure of their personal past lessened but did not cease. It is likely it never will, at least not until fallout from the Iraq War and rumblings about further conflicts in the region disappear from the international landscape – an unlikely possibility in anything like the foreseeable future.

But for now, the Guns were in a quieter space, looking around them, wondering where to begin building a normal life.

They began with the ordinary.

Yasar's job had become increasingly pressure-filled. He was working long, difficult hours just to provide the barest essentials in a country where the cost of living is extremely high. The new house, purchased with help from the Harwoods, needed furnishings, and the Metro was not in good mechanical condition. Katharine began searching for work.

A series of jobs, not one of which fitted Katharine's rather unique professional background, seemed at first to provide a solution to growing financial problems. But never for long. The jobs were temporary, nothing permanent, nothing offering a future, contracts that helped for a time. When applying for a more appropriate permanent position, she often found that she was considered 'overqualified'.

Katharine told the authors, 'I am still spending most of my time at home either online or being a housewife. It is very leisurely, but I know it is not helping my state of mind and confidence levels.' It did not help financially.

What did help, at least in terms of spirit, was the invitation to American University's whistle-blower seminar. With the immigration problem resolved, Katharine was finally able to accept.

'Good news, good news, good news!!!' she wrote to Ray McGovern. 'We are now legitimate citizens! I am now pretty sure that I will be able to come to the United States – as long as they don't arrest me at the border! So, you can book those tickets. I am ready,' she assured, 'to rock and roll.'

Katharine returned home from an exhilarating visit and a roster of new and supportive international friends to a renewed UK celebrity, which did nothing to ease the problem of earning a decent living, a problem she never thought she would have. She was a university graduate with excellent work experience. She had a career. She had had a life. But things were different now.

Excerpts from letters reveal just how different from her life before her arrest:

'I spoke with a lady from the BBC the other day, she just wanted to meet me and chat about the possibilities of doing either a drama documentary about my case or following some new line of information from people who have contacted me because of the truth-telling project. She has approached her manager with the idea of a drama and will reply when she has more details.'

And another example:

'I was approached by IPA [Institute for Public Accuracy] to be a contact on their news release re the indictment story. So far, two radio stations have contacted me about doing an interview on Monday. I don't know if they'll both happen, but as usual, I'm slightly nervous about going on air! I'm almost always nervous, it seems.'

Requests for interviews came not just from the United Kingdom, but also from the United States, including New York, Atlanta, and Phoenix. Interviewers, she said, were 'really supportive and wonderful'. But of a North Carolina interviewer she wrote, 'He was quite antagonistic, and I didn't expect that at all. I don't know if it was his personal opinion or whether he was playing devil's advocate, but he was certainly doing a damn good job if it was the latter. I felt that I really had to defend my position and the whole anti-war mentality. It was a bit uncomfortable, but I hope I got my point across. It's always easy to preach to the converted, so hopefully I may have induced some people to rethink their positions.'

And later, 'Yesterday, I did an interview for a Greek TV channel. The hot topic in Greece at the moment is the bugging of the Olympic committee. The programme is going to compare that with previous buggings, like Watergate and my story.'

The week following the Greek programme, Katharine spoke to the National Union of Journalists with *Observer* editor Martin Bright; their topic was the Official Secrets Act.

Media attention did not bring financial rewards. A journalist friend told Katharine he thought she had a talent for writing, and she began doing articles – principally on Iraq. She hoped doing so would help financially and make her hours 'spent at home with my laptop' more productive.

The Gun marriage was healthy, despite every reason for it not to be, despite the real-life roller coaster their lives had become. Testing the relationship were difficulties more compelling than lack of money, employment problems, and the pressure of media attention. Most significant was the unsettling change in personal relationships. Closest friends remained loyal and supportive, but they were very few, and reinforcing social activities were dramatically curtailed. Once surrounded by colleagues in the intelligence community, Katharine was now very much alone in terms of professional contact, except for a very few GCHQ staffers who dared to continue a friendship with her. And Yasar, the vibrant Mediterranean, was dealing with a sense of suffocation in the cool atmosphere of England.

Katharine found herself more and more concerned about her husband's homesickness: 'It occurred to me yesterday that we should save up for a real visit with his family. Each time he speaks on the phone to his mum, she ends up crying and asking him to come home. It breaks his heart. It shouldn't be a problem now that his status is valid here and he can travel without worry. Perhaps it is something we can aim for some time next year. His parents aren't getting any younger, that's for sure.'

Despite 'being legal', the thought of going abroad likely always will bring with it just a tinge of concern about safe travel and safe return. The prize, this trip to Turkey, seemed worth the emotional price (forget the financial). When it finally happened, Katharine wrote:

'You will be happy to hear that we are safely in Turkey. We got here with no problem at all, which was a huge relief. We were awake for over forty hours due to travelling at funny times of the night, but the pace is so relaxed here that Yasar feels quite at ease.

'Yasar's family are lovely, very welcoming. They live in quite humble surroundings, but it's a nice, friendly environment. We've just been spending the day walking around and greeting all Yasar's old friends in town, having lots of cups of tea (which Yasar tells me is good for me in hot weather).

'There were a lot of tears when we arrived yesterday. Yasar was crying more than anyone else. Please don't worry.'

Katharine wrote of a beautiful country and beautiful people, of nights sleeping on the roof to take advantage of fresh, cool breezes. Deliberately, they distanced themselves – and still do – from Turkish political issues.

At home once again, Katharine finally found employment that was satisfying and appropriate – teaching Chinese. It was (and still is) only part-time, but she enjoys every moment in the classroom. She also has designed simple language lessons for a general audience, lessons she hopes to market in newspaper or magazine format.

Katharine writes:

'The lessons have been going well. I have nineteen for the evening class and five for the afternoon one. As long as the total is over twenty-one, both classes will be viable, so I'm excited about that and the extra bit of cash that will be coming in. My evening class is mostly youngsters, a lot of them are my age or younger, but there are also a couple of over-fifties. The afternoon class is somewhat older, although not by much. The slightly strange thing is that two of the ladies in the afternoon are from GCHQ; in fact, I know one of them, not well, but her name was familiar and when I saw her, I realized that I did know her. I just carry on as if our paths have never crossed.

'Apparently, a French teacher at the college teaches about five people from GCHQ, and when they had their first class, one of them said "One of us is one of you," the French lady asked, "Oh? What do they teach?" and when she learned that it was Chinese, she immediately realized that they were talking about me. When she told me, I felt quite sad, the fact that they still refer to me as "one of them" . . . I don't know how widespread that feeling is; it's almost as if once an intelligence officer, always an intelligence officer.

'I liked the community feeling at GCHQ, the sense of belonging you get working at that place, but I can't condone everything they do. When I go to teach, the college buildings are a stone's throw away from the new "doughnut" GCHQ. Funny that.

'I am enjoying the classes. Everyone I've met in the foreign languages department is lovely. I'm taking Turkish on Tuesday afternoons so I'm in the department three days a week. Starting soon I'll be taking the Certificate for Further Education Training, which will continue for several months and takes place once a week. I'm looking forward to doing that as well.'

At the time Katharine wrote these words, her husband was back visiting his family in Turkey. Lonely, missing him terribly, Katharine prepared for his return with the eagerness of a child waiting for Santa. Except that the gift giving would be reversed.

'Hubby is coming home tomorrow! I'm so excited. I got all prepared last weekend. Thinking that he would be back last Tuesday, I bought this piece of pink cloth with little hearts and kisses on it and wrapped some little presents up which I was going to hide around the house for him to find when he came home.

'One day when we were at the beach in Turkey, he went off diving to the bottom of the water and resurfaced with a stone the shape of a heart. He gave it to me and I've kept it by my side ever since, so I wrapped that up, too. Ah well, I'll be here to welcome him home now, so that's all that matters.'

Not all that mattered. Katharine and Yasar wanted a child, but it took a while for her to become pregnant; possibly, they think, because of all the stress that had so filled their lives. When it finally happened, she wrote of her condition and the continuing financial issues that shadowed it:

'I am now ten weeks pregnant. I'm extremely lucky that I don't suffer from sickness. My mum didn't and had two very smooth, easy births (except that Mike was nearly two months early), but apart from that, easy births seem to run in the family (fingers crossed). In the first few weeks I was definitely grumpy, moody and very tired. Poor Mum had the brunt of that since she was here right around that period. It now seems to have lifted, and I have more energy than I've had for ages and generally feel quite optimistic.

'Ma says that the pregnancy hormones tend to cocoon a woman and prevent her from worrying. They seem to be doing the trick now, but while she was here, I did have a panic over our finances. She reminded me that our mortgage payments would be going up this summer, and after calculating what our essential outgoings are, it made me realize that we can't really afford a leap in mortgage payments. I think dealing with finances is incredibly difficult, especially when the man is doing all he can and working like the devil. Still, at the moment, "cocooned", I'm not letting myself worry.

'On the positive side, my employer is very helpful and said that I could certainly take a term or more off from teaching if that fitted better. Most of my department colleagues are women and a lot of them are mothers, so I'm sure I'll get plenty of advice and support there.

'I have a scan in about two weeks which will be my first. That will be really exciting, and hopefully Yasar will be able to bunk off work for a few hours to see the scan. I think it must make it so much more real when you can see the little wiggly thing in your belly.'

Katharine's next letter was tragic:

'I had a miscarriage yesterday/today and the pregnancy is over. It was confirmed at the hospital this morning. I'm all right, just coming to terms and of course I've had a good cry . . . I'm thinking that it's nature's way, and perhaps it just wasn't the right time.'

There was the miscarriage and then a devastating flood, one that washed through their house destroying floors and furniture and wreaking a havoc that moved them out of their home for months. The present was nearly unbearable and the future far from promising.

And then, unexpectedly, there was reason for hope, a small but tentatively viable reason. Katharine was once again expecting a child. She continued to teach and took leave when the baby was due. Yasar, who had yet to find the kind of employment that was both economically and emotionally satisfying, was thrilled at the prospect of becoming a father.

Katharine wrote to the authors in February 2008:

'Gong Xi Fa Cai (pronounced gong shee fa tsai). That's the proper Mandarin Chinese greeting for New Year. This lunar new year, which starts tomorrow, is the year of the Golden Rat. In college tonight all the language teachers were gathered around as we figured out which animal of the Chinese zodiac we were.

'I'm a tiger, the French teacher is an ox and so on. I don't think I'm much of a tiger, but this stands out (bearing in mind what's happened in the last 5 years!): "Tigers like people, involvement, and dedication to humanitarian causes. They seek out adventures, and at certain points in their lives, they will be very rebellious. They must act out some of their ideals and lash out at the wrongs of society".'

Sounds a lot like Katharine Gun.

EPILOGUE: Reflecting on 31 January 2003

The implication is that the intelligence threat from the United States is also rising by the day.[1]
> – From a January 2008 Chinese intelligence analysis

There is no longer a realistic prospect of a conviction in this [the Pasquill OSA] case.
> – Crown Prosecutor Mark Ellison

T HE MORE THINGS change . . .

In January 2008, exactly four years after Frank Koza e-mailed GCHQ, there were indications – despite warnings and lessons of universal import – that some things were impervious to change. This, regardless of a horrendous and controversial war, reorganization after reorganization of the often contentious and competing US intelligence entities and agencies, and promises of adherence to international accords. In the United Kingdom, although Tony Blair had been replaced by Gordon Brown, there continued serious grumbling about Iraq and concomitant concern about US influence, further revelations about government hanky-panky, and the same old battles over the inefficacy of the Official Secrets Act.

Just two pithy examples, happenings reported within days of each other on the fourth anniversary of the NSA misadventure:

In China, the government-controlled media reported an intelligence expert's complaint that the US National Security Agency was spying on his country's electronic communications. The expert was reacting in kind. An American media report had claimed that Chinese intelligence penetrated the NSA's Kunia listening post in Hawaii through a 'translation service'. Mandarin translators, like Katharine Gun during her days at GCHQ in Cheltenham, do this sort of thing daily, sharing with the NSA. The spy in the sky game continues, and it would be ridiculously naïve to suggest it does not or should not.

Further, the Chinese were not happy about what was happening in Kunia, observing that the Hawaiian listening post was steadily growing in size and power.

Also in January 2008, a London Foreign Office civil servant starred in a high drama at the Old Bailey that had tongues wagging about a re-enactment of the Katharine Gun case. The prosecutor replaying his earlier role was Mark Ellison, in charge as the Crown lost yet another high-profile OSA case. Charges against Derek Pasquill were suddenly dropped when it came to light that even his own senior officers had claimed his leaking Whitehall documents did no harm.[2] Included in the leak was information about US secret transport of terror suspects to foreign countries where they could be tortured.

It was rumoured that the case was dropped because to continue would have caused the UK government serious embarrassment. Of course, this was said about the failed case against Katharine, where the embarrassment would have been far greater. In both, the reason given was failure of a realistic chance of conviction. As for US embarrassment, the American public already knew of the practice of 'extraordinary rendition' because of leaked documents.

Whistle-blower David Shayler, furious about his failure to get charges against him dropped and the fact that he served six months in prison, told the world that the reason the OSA charges prevailed against him was because dropping the charges would have caused political humiliation for the government. This was no way to mete out justice, steamed Shayler.

And then the *Observer* called for reform of the Official Secrets Act. So, why was what began on 31 January 2003 at America's National Security Agency so very important at the time and why is it still important?

Most significantly, much of the world learned then (and afterwards, in America) how and why the ill-conceived spy operation helped kill a UN Security Council resolution legitimizing the strike against Iraq. It would learn that the NSA, despite claims to the contrary, may not always be careful about complying with the law, that it may add to its sin of playing horrendous 'dirty tricks' on international friends by lying about such matters. It wasn't the listening, it was the lying, and it was the intent to steal UNSC votes. Information worth knowing.

Even in April 2007, as director of the Central Intelligence Agency reflecting back on his NSA leadership role, Michael Hayden told CSPAN's Brian Lamb that the agency works only within the confines of the law, within 'what's legally permitted'. Compliance with the law, all laws, is essential and inviolable. This has been his claim all along, despite what seems to be evidence to the contrary. It raises a question of trust. In December of the same year, Hayden was busy defending destruction of CIA interrogation tapes of terrorist suspects, telling agency employees that the recordings were destroyed [despite legal warning not to do so] to protect the identities of interrogators.[3] It is not unreasonable to question his veracity in this regard.

Spin attributed failure to secure a resolution for war solely to the possibility of a veto by permanent members of the Security Council, but this was not true – 'freedom fries' publicity notwithstanding. Further, possibility was not yet reality. Had the swing nations, the targets named in the NSA e-mail, voted in favour of adoption, there was at least the hope that George Bush and Tony Blair would prevail and the resolution might succeed. But instead, those nations were outraged and insulted, and hope vanished into diplomatic ether with Katharine Gun's leak. The United States had gone too far.

Had the 31 January event not happened, even if the resolution had later been vetoed, Security Council approval would likely have paid off in the currency of a broader coalition for, and greater international acceptance of, the war. Public relations value would have been enormous.

Facing inevitable defeat, the two world leaders withdrew the resolution and had to find another road to Baghdad. And that's where they got into serious trouble. That's where Elizabeth Wilmshurst and Robin Cook and Clare Short, standing on principle, bailed out of Tony Blair's government. In the United States, defeat led to manipulation of intelligence in support of an illegal war, and even to deceiving members of Congress.

The 31 January event, of course, was responsible for the arrest of a young woman who defended her action as a matter of conscience and, in spite of everything that happened, would 'do it again'. Here was a concept worth thinking about. It was so important that dozens of news articles and interviews and discussions focused on it. The words 'I have only ever followed my conscience' appeared everywhere. 'I would do it again' was the commitment printed across the cheek of a full-page *Guardian* photograph of Katharine's face.

Katharine's fealty to conscience and willingness to repeat her offence led to her being nominated, along with other high-profilers (ironically including Condoleezza Rice), as a 2004 'International Woman of the Year'.[4] Like it or not, she became a personal-ethic role model and remains one today. It was not just what Katharine Gun had done, but why that was so important. Her conscience told her she had to prevent a war and the death and maiming of thousands of innocent lives. Responding to its insistence, she tattled on the establishment and risked everything. She was a leaker.

She was also a leader, a fact that pleased some and sickened others.

Spring of 2005 opened one of the wettest political seasons ever, with devastating intelligence leaks flooding both the United States and the United Kingdom, a deluge revealing behind-the-scenes deceptions and manipulations in the run-up to war. What Katharine Gun did two years earlier proved to be a fatal crack in a carefully guarded international dam of secrecy. That first critical leak inspired those that followed. She has been instrumental in a surge of interest in truth telling in and about government.

Given the complexity of profound international issues and challenges, like the 'Iran problem', Katharine's invitation to government workers to leak this sort of information may well bear fruit in the months and years ahead. 'Follow me' has been her clarion call. This can be a frightening prospect, perhaps even anarchistic, or it can be a tool for universal good. 31 January put a different face on the United Nations and the electronic miasma in which it operates. There is much that does not work in that august body, much that needs to be changed if there is hope that it will function in the way intended. What does work, however, is the extensive bugging operation that has plagued the institution since its birth in San Francisco more than a half-century ago.

Insiders know that everyone has always spied on everyone else at the United Nations, so what makes this case different? For one thing, it extended to non-insiders knowledge that international diplomacy as practised at the supposedly sacrosanct United Nations isn't always diplomatic at its best, and is illegal at its worst. It started with people, ordinary people, wondering whether a new ethic might lead to transparency and honesty at the impressive building overlooking New York's East River. Just because spying has always been a part of the United Nations' history does not mean it must be a part of its future. Everything else aside, it might be rather agreeable to honour international agreements in this regard. Here is another concept worth thinking about.

What was most shocking about this sorry spying blunder, and still is, was the intent behind it. The United States was so determined to get its way that it was willing to collect private information for what at least appears to be a bit of high-stakes blackmail. President Bush had said he was willing to do most anything, to 'twist arms' to get what he wanted, and this was one strong-armed, clay-footed way of doing so. Would an American president resort to this sort of bully tactic today? If so, is someone going to be willing to let the political cat out of the bag? And should he or she do so?

A question of special significance is this: How can citizens know, today, when disgraceful political bullying or deliberate manipulation of intelligence happens in their country? When it happens in America, a nation long considered captain of the Good Ship Morality, an international law-abider, an arbiter of global ethics? They cannot always know, but whistle-blowing helps in creating a less gullible coast-to-coast community.

As for America's image abroad, it is apparent that something sad has happened, has changed its character, has tarnished it. There is no question that the NSA plot to steal the UN Security Council vote contributed to its corrosion.

The bogeyman that Frank Koza released on 31 January 2003 did considerable damage. It did not, however, destroy the essence of hope for a political life properly conducted, although it toyed with the national psyche, raised international concerns, and messed with trust of government.

In the United Kingdom, this same mythical character re-ignited controversy over the provisions and effectiveness of the Official Secrets Act when Katharine Gun walked away free. The act has been called 'draconian' and unfair to those wishing to do what Katharine Gun did in responding to her conscience.

'The sum of these concerns strongly suggests that . . . the Official Secrets Act, as it stands, is no longer fit for purpose either to guarantee the protection of confidences or guarantee the human rights of individuals charged under the act,' said the *Observer* in its 13 January 2007 opinion. On a disappointing note, the article says that promises about re-examination of the act have not been kept.

Even before Katharine's arrest, Liberty had called for reform of the act, in a well-worded bit of prescience: 'The current secrecy laws are far too restrictive; they encourage abuse. Reforms need to ensure proper judicial scrutiny of any restriction on people's freedom of expression or information.' Protecting national security is important, Liberty said, but a balance was needed between that interest and the public's right to freedom of information.

As times become more threatening, as terrorist activity continues to explode around the world, protecting national security must be a top priority. The NSA operation was conducted under the blanket of national security; in the end, it did nothing to protect but a great deal to provoke.

Perhaps it was only one of the abuses in its name, abuses paid for with individual and international rights.

As Liberty observed two years before taking on the pro bono case of the young Katharine Gun, 'National security needs to be properly and tightly defined.'[5] On 31 January 2003, the NSA proved Liberty's point.

ACKNOWLEDGEMENTS

THE AUTHORS ARE grateful to a number of fine people whose wisdom and support were invaluable in researching and writing this book.

In the United Kingdom: Katharine and Yasar Gun, who told their story well and without violating restrictions imposed by the Official Secrets Act; James Welch, brilliant Liberty solicitor; Martin Bright, political editor of the *New Statesman* and former courageous home affairs editor of the *Observer*; the Right Honourable Clare Short, member of Parliament and former Blair cabinet minister, who spoke with fire and conviction; Elizabeth Wilmshurst, former Foreign Office deputy legal adviser and respected international law expert; two special people from the intelligence community – Glenmore Trenear-Harvey, intelligence analyst, and Nigel West, noted writer and former member of Parliament; gracious Paul and Jan Harwood; crusading journalist Yvonne Ridley; and Ava Astaire and Richard McKenzie, who made their London home our own.

In the United States and Canada: The erudite Honorable Edward Bayda, retired Chief Justice, Saskatchewan; Norman Solomon, noted journalist and author, whose support has been invaluable; Daniel Ellsberg, whistle-blower icon; Ray McGovern, veteran intelligence analyst and former CIA officer; Sean Penn, actor–peace activist; Marsha Coleman-Adebayo, whistle-blower and dedicated activist; Robert Lutz, highly successful corporate executive and former Marine attack pilot; Dr Peter O. Whitmer, author, clinical psychologist, keen observer of human behaviour; Patricia Lebrun, educator and fine reviewer; Lorraine and Judd Horbaly, supporters and organizers of a focus group to review the partial manuscript; Peggy Adler, energetic supporter, organizer, and intelligence researcher; Mary Yost, agent and friend.

In getting the manuscript ready for publication, thanks go to Tom Killingbeck and Eleanor Bishop at HarperCollins; and Benjamin Arden and Richard Huffman for legal support. This Second Edition was inspired by the making of *Official Secrets*, the feature film made from this volume. The production team included producers Ged Doherty and Elizabeth Fowler, director Gavin Hood, screenwriters Gregory Bernstein and Sara Bernstein, and distributors EntertainmentOne and IFC. The First Edition was published with PoliPoint Press: Scott Jordan, Peter Richardson, Melissa Edeburn; BookMatters, Dave Peattie; and masterful copyeditor Edith Gladstone.

Close to home, which makes them last but certainly not least, Kristin Donnan, ever faithful and dedicated editor and agent of her mother's work; Lynn Eyermann, invaluable in First Edition support; and Judy Duhamel and Ann Thompson, for reasons they know.

– Marcia and Tom Mitchell, 20 February 2008
(with additions by Marcia, exactly eleven years later)

NOTES

FOREWORD

1. While the Iraq Inquiry Report was not positioned to judge the war's legal status, it raised serious questions about its legality. Specifically, it concluded that the circumstances in which it was ultimately decided that there was a legal basis for UK participation were far from satisfactory. Executive Summary, 62–69.
2. Brown, Gordon. *My Life, Our Times* (London: Random House UK, 2017).

THE KOZA MEMO

1. Text is copied from the original document. Other sources may include changes to the original.

CHAPTER 1

1. Michael Hayden, address to the National Press Club, Washington, DC, 23 January 2006.
2. Michael Hayden, interview with Kwame Holman, 17 May 2006.
3. James Bamford, *Body of Secrets: Anatomy of the Ultra-Secret NSA* (New York: Doubleday, 2001), 456.

CHAPTER 2

1. Interview with the authors.
2. Matthew Rycroft, memo to David Manning, UK Cabinet Office briefing paper, 23 July 2002.

CHAPTER 3

1. Martin Bright, interview with the authors, London, June 2005.
2. Martin Bright and Peter Beaumont, 'Britain spied on UN allies over war vote', *Observer,* 8 February 2004.
3. UK Cabinet Office briefing paper, 'Iraq: Conditions for Military Action', 21 July 2002.
4. Maggie Farley and Richard Bourdreaux, 'Mexico's Envoy to UN Leaves, with Defiance', *Los Angeles Times,* 23 November 2003.
5. Yvonne Ridley's quoted statements throughout come from e-mail messages to the authors, February 2008.
6. Bright interview.

CHAPTER 4

1. In early 2003 the solicitor John Wadham was director of Liberty, the human rights organization that would represent Katharine Gun.

CHAPTER 5

1. 'Harris poll undermines media's excuses for ignoring new evidence of Bush falsehoods in lead-up to Iraq War', *Media Matters for America,* 26 July 2006, http://mediamatters.org/items/200607260005.
2. Clare Short, *An Honourable Deception* (London: Simon and Schuster, 2004), 92.

3. Jason Vest, 'Saddam in the Crosshairs', *Village Voice*, 20 November 2001, http://www.villagevoice.com/issues/0147/vest.php.

4. Clare Short, personal interview with the authors, Portcullis House, London, 9 June 2005.

5. 'Iraq: Conditions for Military Action' (see Note 3, Chapter 3).

6. Ibid.

7. Michael Smith, 'UK Foreign Office paper leak', *Irish Sunday Times*, 19 June 2005.

8. Justifying the pre-emptive strike against Iraq, apologists cite Clinton's failure to deal decisively with Saddam.

9. Rycroft, memo to Manning (see Note 2, Chapter 2).

10. Ibid.

11. Andrew Woodcock, 'Scarlett "Asked Experts to Harden Weapons Hunt Report",' *Scotsman,* 4 August 2004.

12. Adolfo Aguilar Zinser, 'Tony and the Truth', BBC *Panorama* documentary, recorded from transmission, 20 March 2005.

13. 'Iraq's Weapons of Mass Destruction: The Assessment of the British Government', also known as 'the September Dossier', released 24 September 2002. A later dossier, 'Iraq: Its Infrastructure of Concealment, Deception and Intimidation', irreverently called 'the Dodgy Dossier', was released 3 February 2003.

14. Robin Cook, 'Blair and Scarlett told me Iraq had no usable weapons', *Guardian* (London), 12 July 2004.

CHAPTER 6

1. Don Cox, 'Reno Restaurateurs Pop Their Corks in Protest', *Reno Gazette Journal,* 26 April 2006.

2. 'Mexican and Chilean diplomats claim Iraq peace efforts were scuppered by British and American intelligence spy operations', *Eye Spy Magazine* (London), no. 24, 18 March 2004.

3. Washington claimed that delay in finalizing the treaty was due to a complex translation process, not to Chile's failure to support a second resolution. See 'Lagos Humiliates Chile by Not Standing Tall over Its Iraq Vote', *Council on Hemispheric Affairs,* 16 May

2003; and Colum Lynch, 'US Threatened Allies in Run-up to Invasion, Chilean Diplomat Says', *Washington Post,* 23 March 2008.

4. The argument as to who was the mastermind was never, to the authors' knowledge, settled.

5. 'Annan, Rice Pay Tribute to Maverick Mexican Envoy', Reuters, 6 June 2005.

6. Herman Etchaleco, 'Chile to Investigate Spying, Denounces US Intelligence Services', *Pravda,* 4 March 2003.

7. Specific complaints about the spy operation are not forthcoming from countries beholden to the United States.

8. Bob Drogin and Greg Miller, 'Purported Spy Memo May Add to US Troubles at UN', *Global Policy Forum,* 4 March 2003.

9. Ibid.

10. 'NZ spy base being used in US dirty tricks check says Locke', *New Zealand Herald,* 4 March 2003.

11. Secret memo to the prime minister from Lord Goldsmith, Section 23, 7 March 2003 (in reference to recording French conversations).

12. 'The real intelligence failure was Blair's and Bush's', *Sunday Herald* (London), 11 July 2004.

13. The thirteen-page opinion of 7 March 2003 listed six caveats, cautions that were wiped out in the brief go-ahead opinion given to Parliament on 17 March 2003.

14. Wilmshurst, also an international law professor at University College London, testified before the Butler Committee on pre-war intelligence.

15. Robin Cook, reported in the *Guardian,* 12 July 2004.

16. Short, *An Honourable Deception,* 212 (see Note 2, Chapter 5).

CHAPTER 8

1. The Harwoods' statements are from interviews with the authors.

2. Founded in 1934, Liberty, the National Council for Civil Liberties, promotes the values of individual human dignity, equal treatment, and fairness as the foundations of a democratic society.

CHAPTER 10

1. Donald Starr, quoted in the *News Telegraph,* 7 August 2005.
2. Ibid.

CHAPTER 11

1. Draft indictment, Bow Street Magistrates Court, *The Queen v. Katharine Teresa Gun,* n.d.
2. Richard Norton-Taylor, 'Woman's lawyers fight to lift GCHQ gag', *Guardian,* 20 January 2004.
3. Molly Ivins, 'Gun Battle', syndicated column, 17 February 2004.

CHAPTER 12

1. Katharine Gun, writing to the authors during this time of stress.

CHAPTER 13

1. J. F. O. McAllister, 'A smoking gun puts the war on trial', *Time* Europe 163, no. 5, 2 February 2004.
2. Ibid.
3. Shayler's case was complicated and included his argument that the absolute bar on disclosure breached Article 10 of the European Convention on Human Rights.
4. 'A Smoking Gun', *News Review* (London), 7 August 2005.
5. Lord Denning: *Southwark London Borough Council v. Williams* (1971), 2 AER 175.
6. David Shayler, 'The case against GCHQ whistle blower exposes glaring flaws in Britain's unwritten constitution', *Observer,* 21 February 2004.
7. Appointment of New DPP, Attorney General's news release, London, 5 August 2003.

8. *Parliamentary Debates,* Lords, 5th series, column 662, 3 March 2004.

CHAPTER 14

1. Surprisingly, news coverage of this statement included the story 'Britain Drops Charges in Leak of US Memo', *New York Times,* 26 February 2004.
2. *R v. Katharine Gun,* Advance Notice of Defence Statement, section 8.
3. Ibid., section 8(b).
4. Ibid., section 9(b).
5. Ibid., section 11.
6. Paxman was famed for pinning Tony Blair (and other dignitaries) to the wall during notoriously tough interviews.

CHAPTER 15

1. Tony Blair, London press conference, 26 February 2004.
2. Statement on *R v. Katharine Gun,* 26 February 2004, 108/04.
3. Reference here is not to the original advice given to Blair on 7 March 2003, but the advice provided ten days later, which found the war legal.
4. Short, 2005 interview with the authors (see Note 4, Chapter 5). (Short made it clear that there was abundant deceit and duplicity concerning the abandonment of the Gun case.)
5. Transcript, daily press briefing by the Office of the Spokesman for the Secretary General, 26 February 2004.
6. Two years later Gen. Michael Hayden, Frank Koza's then supervisor at NSA, would make the same claim while touring congressional offices in support of his nomination to head the CIA.
7. 'Blix had mobile phone tapped by allied spies', *Telegraph,* 27 February 2004.

8. Secret memo to the prime minister from Lord Goldsmith, Section 36, 7 March 2003.
9. Robin Cook, reported in the *Guardian,* 12 July 2004.

CHAPTER 17

1. Robin Cook, 'Blair and Scarlett told me Iraq had no usable weapons' (see Note 14, Chapter 5).
2. Robert Lutz, personal interview with the authors, January 2008.
3. Feature cover, *Guardian,* 26 February 2004.
4. Peter Whitmer, personal interview with the authors, 22 February 2008.
5. Tony Blair, the prime minister's introduction to the September Dossier, 'Iraq's Weapons of Mass Destruction' (see Note 13, Chapter 5).

CHAPTER 18

1. Katharine Gun, 'The truth must out', *Observer,* 19 September 2004, and reiterated with slight variation two years later to the authors.
2. Daniel Ellsberg, 'Time to Leak', *Tom Paine Common Sense,* 20 March 2006. Also reiterated in a telephone conversation with M. Mitchell in 2005.
3. 'UK Involved in Espionage Against Iran', *Association of Former Intelligence Officers Newsletter,* 14 December 2007.
4. In August 2000 a jury found the EPA guilty of race, sex, and colour discrimination and of creating a hostile work environment against Coleman-Adebayo. Since then, she has become a leading spokesperson for whistle-blowing.
5. Ben Davies, BBC News, 15 September 2004.
6. In March 2007 the House passed H. 985, and in November the Senate would pass S. 274, providing critical whistle-blower reforms for US federal workers.

7. Whistle-blower hero Sam Adams discovered in 1967 that there were more than twice the number of Vietnamese Communists under arms than the United States claimed.

8. As a result of Grevil's leak, Prime Minister Anders Fogh Rasmussen ordered declassification of pre-war intelligence documents to a public now doubting the government's credibility.

9. Greg Gordon, Washington bureau correspondent, *Star Tribune*, 9 September 2004.

10. Daniel Ellsberg, 'About the Truth-Telling Project', www.ellsberg. net/truthtelling project.

11. Ray McGovern, 'Mary McCarthy's Choice', *Tom Paine Common Sense*, 24 April 2006.

EPILOGUE

1. *Association of Former Intelligence Officers Newsletter*, 14 January 2006; from the *World Tribune*, 8 January 2008. Originally quoted from *Beijing Qingnian Cankao* (Elite Reference).

2. Pasquill was arrested two years earlier and charged in September 2007 with six counts of violation of the OSA.

3. Reported by the Associated Press, 19 December 2007.

4. 'Women of the Year,' *Guardian*, 12 December 2004.

5. Liberty, press release, London, 10 September 2001.

INDEX

Abrams, Elliott, 55
Afghanistan, US/UK invasion, 29–30
Aguilar Zinser, Adolfo, 29, 34, 62, 70–1, 73
Akram, Munir, 74
Alvear, Soledad, 71
Anderson, Donald, 174
Angola, 7, 16, 51, 75, 84
Annan, Kofi, 74, 160, 161, 162, 187
Arias, Inocencio, 72
Armitage, Richard L., 55

Baker, James, 73
Beaumont, Peter, 32, 34, 41
Biden, Joe, 84–5
Birmingham, University of, 103–04, 124
Blair, Tony: accusations of intelligence misuse, 99, 102, 136, 195; and bugging of Kofi Annan, 162–3; Robin Cook on conduct of, 77, 178, 189; and democratic principles, 129; deploys naval task force to Gulf, 64; Gun case shakes government of, 87, 136–7, 140–1, 153–4, 155–6, 165–7, 176–85; legal advice given to *see* Goldsmith, Lord (Attorney General); meeting with Bush at

Crawford, 28, 57–8, 60, 190; motivations of, 179, 185–6, 190; Oval Office meeting, 12–3, 64–6; public rhetoric of, 17, 18, 27–8, 57; secret road map to war, 2, 17, 28, 34, 51–5, 57–61, 63–7; Clare Short's criticisms of, 79; Rowan Williams on, 75; worries over Bush regime's aggression, 56–7, 185
Bletchley Park, 12
Blix, Hans, 20, 164
Bolton, John, 55, 59
Bright, Martin, 25, 30–33, 34, 41, 81, 86, 157–8, 205
Brown, Gordon, 5, 211
Brownfield, William, 72
Bulgaria, 7, 16, 51, 74, 84
Burnett, John, 173–4
Bush, George W.: autistic extremism of, 184–5; declassified correspondence with Blair, 2; and democratic principles, 128; deploys US troops to Gulf, 64; desire to be 'war president', 184; and doctrine of pre-emption, 59, 62; hanging chads in Florida, 189; intent behind UN spying operation, 15, 17, 18–20,

ABOUT THE AUTHORS

MARCIA MITCHELL is a former associate director of the American Film Institute, and a former senior executive for the Corporation for Public Broadcasting. She was the first female member of the South Dakota Governor's Cabinet, serving as Secretary of Labor. She began her career as a journalist and won both state and national press awards for writing and editing. She has received critical acclaim for her non-fiction books. Her recent work in mystery fiction is an exciting new literary adventure for her. She has served on numerous boards and commissions concerned with women's issues, the arts, and the humanities.

TOM MITCHELL served as a Special Agent of the FBI for seventeen years, during which time he supervised counter-intelligence investigations in New York. During his later years in the Bureau, he worked closely with FBI Director J. Edgar Hoover. Throughout his career in intelligence, Tom was associated with some of the country's most famous espionage and criminal cases. He transitioned from the world of intrigue to the world of commerce and retired as a vice president of Georgia-Pacific Corporation. Tom died on 15 March 2010.

Tom's extensive background in intelligence and Marcia's background in writing and research led to the Mitchells' first book together, *The Spy Who Seduced America: Lies and Betrayal in the*

Heat of the Cold War. Through Tom's contacts, the Mitchells twice travelled to Moscow to meet with KGB (now FSB) contacts. From there, the couple travelled to the United Kingdom in search of the truth surrounding the Katharine Gun story. Over the years, the Mitchells addressed audiences throughout the United States and were honoured to speak at an intelligence seminar at Cambridge University. Their work in the area of intelligence has resulted in continuing relationships with former and present members of US, UK, Canadian, and Russian intelligence services, as well as with other intelligence 'insiders'.